ALPHA
CENTAURI,
THE
NEAREST
STAR

Books on Astronomy by
ISAAC ASIMOV

THE CLOCK WE LIVE ON
THE KINGDOM OF THE SUN
THE DOUBLE PLANET
ENVIRONMENTS OUT THERE
THE UNIVERSE
TO THE ENDS OF THE UNIVERSE
JUPITER, THE LARGEST PLANET
ASIMOV ON ASTRONOMY
OUR WORLD IN SPACE
EYES ON THE UNIVERSE
ALPHA CENTAURI, THE NEAREST STAR

For young readers

THE MOON
MARS
STARS
GALAXIES
COMETS AND METEORS
THE SUN
ABC'S OF SPACE
WHAT MAKES THE SUN SHINE?
THE SOLAR SYSTEM
HOW DID WE FIND OUT ABOUT COMETS?

ALPHA CENTAURI,

THE NEAREST STAR

ISAAC ASIMOV

Lothrop, Lee & Shepard Company
A Division of William Morrow & Company, Inc. • *New York*

2   3   4   5   6   7   8   9   10

Library of Congress Cataloging in Publication Data

Asimov, Isaac, [date]
    Alpha Centauri, the nearest star.

    SUMMARY: Discusses the constellations and stars, the distance, luminosity and size, stellar astronomy, starlight, and life on other planetary systems, with special reference to the third brightest and also the nearest star, Alpha Centauri.
    1. Alpha Centauri—Juvenile literature.   2. Stars—Juvenile literature.
[1. Alpha Centauri.   2.   Stars.   3.   Astronomy]   I.   Title.
QB805.A84   523.8   76-29037
ISBN 0-688-41779-5
ISBN 0-688-51779-X lib. bdg.

CONTENTS

LIST
OF
TABLES

1
THE
CONSTELLATIONS

The Moon's Motion

Imagine a dark, cloudless night in some country area where there are no city lights and no highway lights. On such a night, you would see the stars in the sky more brightly and in greater numbers than one can possibly see them under ordinary conditions in many places today.

You would see many hundreds of them, some bright and some faint, in different patterns. If you watched every night, you might begin to recognize some of the patterns—two bright stars close together here, a group of seven stars that look like a ladle there, three medium-bright stars in a line with two brighter stars above and two brighter stars below in still another place.

You might notice that the patterns always stay the same night after night, year after year. You might notice that particular patterns shift position each night. A particular group of stars might be near the eastern horizon at nightfall. Each following night at the same time, the group would be higher in the sky until it was as high as it could be, and then it would move down to the western horizon.

Eventually, it wouldn't be visible at all at nightfall, because it would be below the western horizon. But then, if you waited long enough it would appear at the eastern horizon again at nightfall. The time it takes for any group of stars to move completely around the sky is 365 days.

But would you watch the stars night after night, so that you would begin to recognize patterns and see how the patterns move? You might watch the sky very closely if it were *useful* to do so. Many years ago, before there were any clocks, people would study the motion of the stars as they marched across the sky. This could give them a notion as to whether it was before or after midnight, and about how long it might be till dawn.

There was something else in the sky that was far more important to people in ancient times than just stars. It was far easier to observe, too. That something was the moon.

The stars are merely points of light, but the moon is a large lighted area. The stars stay the same in appearance night after night, but the moon changes shape. It is a round circle of light at times, but at other times it is a half circle or a thin crescent.

There is just one moon, so it is much easier to watch and study it than it is to try to watch hundreds upon hundreds of stars. The moon is much larger and brighter than any star, and the change in shape is fascinating. It would seem certain that people watched the moon at night before they paid much detailed attention to the stars.

You don't have to watch the moon very long before you see that it changes shape in a regular way. You may see it low in the western sky some night just after sunset; it is a thin crescent and you can just barely make it out. What's more, it is setting and disappears beyond the western horizon not long after the sun does.

The next night it is a thicker crescent; it is higher in the sky and sets later. The night after that it is a thicker crescent still. After seven nights it is a half circle of light, directly overhead at sunset, and doesn't set till about midnight. It is then at the "half-moon" stage.

The moon continues to grow thicker each night, and to be

farther from the sun at sunset. Finally, fourteen days after it first appeared in the western sky as a crescent, it is a complete circle of light, a "full moon" and is so far from the sun that it is rising in the east as the sun sets in the west.

After that the moon is not in the sky at all at sunset. It is so far from the sun that it is beyond the eastern horizon. It does rise, of course—later and later each night—and as the nights progress it is thinner and thinner. Finally, it rises as a half moon again at about midnight.

It continues to rise later and later and to grow thinner and thinner until it is a thin crescent again that rises just at dawn, not long before the sun rises. A couple of days later, the crescent moon shows up low in the west just after sunset and the whole thing starts all over again. People talk of a "new moon" when that crescent in the west first appears.

The moon seems to make a complete circuit of the sky, starting near the sun and coming back to the sun. As it does so it goes through its phases: from new moon, to half moon, to full moon, and back to half moon, and new moon. It takes about twenty-nine and one-half days for the moon to make its complete circle in the sky from new moon back to new moon, and this period of time is called a "month."

Why is this important? Because the moon was the first calendar human beings ever had (and is still the basis of the Jewish and Moslem calendars today).

There are certain cycles of seasons. There are rainy seasons and dry seasons, warm seasons and cold seasons, times when game is plentiful and times when it is not, times when you can expect to get fruit on trees and bushes and times when you can't.

These seasons repeat themselves in regular fashion. In primeval times, people who were able to keep track of this repetition and know when to expect each change could prepare better for new conditions and live more comfortably and well.

This remained true after people learned how to be farmers:

to plant crops and reap a harvest. They had to know when the best time to plant was, and when the harvest might be expected. To be a good farmer, you had to understand the changes of the seasons and be able to foresee them.

It turned out that every twelve months (plus a little extra) the seasons began to repeat. Those twelve months made up a year. In early times, people would watch eagerly for each new moon and celebrate its appearance with a religious festival. They would count the new moons so they would know exactly how to run their farms and their lives in accordance with the seasons.

As the moon went through its cycle of changes in the course of the month, it changed position against the stars. One night it might be near some particular group of stars, but the next night it would be farther east near a neighboring group, and the next night still farther east and so on.

Even people who were not willing to study the stars for their own sake would consider it important to study them if it yielded understanding of the motions of the moon. It is in this way, through a study of the motions of the moon, that astronomy may have begun. The first important astronomers that left written records were in Sumeria, a land located in what is now southern Iraq, about four to five thousand years ago.

Sumerian astronomers found it useful to take notice of about twenty-eight groups of stars ("moon stations") along the moon's path. The moon would move from one group on one night to the next group the night after, and so on. A quick look at the moon in the night sky would then tell them how many days since the last new moon and how many till the next.

The Sun and the Zodiac

The moon isn't a perfect calendar, however. If you count twelve months, each from new moon to new moon, you end up with 354 days. The cycle of seasons takes longer. A new spring starts every 365¼ days (on the average). If you planted your seeds at a certain new moon, then when twelve months had passed and you planted them again, you would be planting them eleven days too soon. By the time you had done this a few times, you would be planting your seeds in midwinter and there would be no harvest.

One way to correct this is to wait until the moon calendar falls about one month behind the seasons and then add an extra month one year so that the moon calendar comes even with the seasons again. This means that some years have twelve months and some years have thirteen months. In fact, a system was eventually worked out in which years were divided up into groups of nineteen, with certain of the group having twelve and certain thirteen and the pattern repeating itself every nineteen years. The ancient Babylonians and Greeks had a calendar like that and the Jewish religious calendar is like that to this day.

Once the early astronomers began marking out moon stations, however, they found that the sun, too, was moving against the stars. Night after night, each moon station was at a slightly different distance from the sun.

The sun followed a circular path around the sky (as measured by its position among the stars), a path that was slightly different from that of the moon. The two paths crossed at two places at opposite sides of the sky. The sun's path eventually came to be called the "ecliptic" because when both the sun and moon happened to reach one of the crossing points at the same time, the moon passed in front of the sun so that there was an eclipse.

When the moon moved around the sky, against the stars, once every 27⅓ days, it did not move from the sun back to the sun. All the while the moon was moving, the sun was moving too, but much more slowly. It took only a little over two days more for the moon to overtake the sun, so that the moon's complete circuit of the sky from sun to sun took 29½ days.

(These little complications in the motion of the moon kept the astronomers on their toes, and that was a good thing. Trying to work out all the details of the moon's motion led them to think about the sun's motion and from that they went on to other things. When something is too easy, people tend to be too easily satisfied, and no progress is made.)

The sun's slower motion means that it takes 365¼ days to go completely around the sky against the background of the stars. The important thing about this is that the time it takes the sun to make a complete circuit of the sky is just the time it takes the seasons to repeat themselves.

If you go by the position of the sun among the moon stations, rather than the position of the moon, you can plant at the same time each year without fail, and harvest at the same time. You can expect the rains to come at the same time each year, or a river to flood.

It was much more practical to tie a calendar to the motions of the sun instead of the moon. Instead of having each month 29 or 30 days long to fit each coming new moon, they could be made 30 or 31 days long so that twelve of them would exactly fit the seasons.

Nevertheless, such a "solar calendar" was not quickly adopted by early people. The "lunar calendar," using the moon, had become so traditional that people didn't like to give it up. The ancient Egyptians were the first to adopt a solar calendar. In 46 B.C. Julius Caesar forced the Romans to adopt the Egyptian calendar.

Meanwhile, even the nations that stuck to a lunar calendar realized the importance of studying the sun's motion. A system of "sun stations" was evolved. The ecliptic was divided into twelve sections. Each section was the distance the sun would move in one month.

Suppose it is in sun station 1 at the time of spring planting. It will move on to sun station 2 the next month, and to sun station 3 the one after, and so on. When it comes back to sun station 1, it is time for planting again.

(You can't actually see what station the sun is in because its glare completely drowns out the stars it is near. You can see nearby sun stations, though, just after sunset and just before dawn, and in that way you can tell what sun station the sun is in—once you've memorized them all.)

Each sun station contains a different pattern of stars and if you know each of the twelve patterns, you have a season calendar of the sky.

Each sun station becomes associated with the star pattern, which is given some dramatic name of an object that can be seen in the pattern. Then it is easy to remember and recognize. Eventually, such a group of stars came to be called a "constellation" from Latin words meaning "stars taken together."

We would say, then, that the sun, as it moves along the ecliptic and makes its circle around the sky, passes through each of twelve constellations, taking one month to pass through one constellation.

The names of the various constellations have come sometimes from familiar animals. In one place along the ecliptic, for instance, there is a group of stars that is curved like an S, rather like a scorpion's body. At one end the stars seem to form a sharp bend like a scorpion's tail, and at the other end, two curves of stars look like claws. Naturally, that constellation is going to be called "Scorpion."

Of course, each nation that studied the constellation with the scorpion pattern would call it by the name of the animal in their own language. Nowadays, however, astronomers of all nations use the Latin word. The Latin word for scorpion is *scorpius*, so that is what we call the constellation. We can say something like "The sun is in Scorpius" and everyone will know what we mean.

In another part of the ecliptic there is a group of stars shaped like a V that reminded people of a bull's head with two long horns. That constellation was called the "Bull." The Latin word for bull is *taurus*, and that is the name of that constellation.

Since many of the constellations along the ecliptic were named for animals, the group of twelve, taken all together, was called *zodiakos* by the Greeks, since that meant, in their language, "a circle of animals." We call it the "zodiac."

The zodiac was worked out in its present form about 450 B.C. by a Greek astronomer named Oenopides (ee-NOP-ih-deez). In Table 1, we have the list of the twelve constellations of the zodiac.

The sun and moon were not the only heavenly bodies whose paths took them through the constellations of the zodiac. There were also five bright star-like objects which moved from constellation to constellation in more complicated paths than those of the sun and moon. The astronomers of each nation gave these bright star-like objects the names of various gods or goddesses whom they worshipped. Today, the official names of the objects, used by astronomers all over the world, are those of Roman gods and goddesses. The five objects are: Mercury, Venus, Mars, Jupiter, and Saturn.

Since the sun, the moon, Mercury, Venus, Mars, Jupiter, and Saturn all moved against the stars and all traced out paths that circled the sky, the Greeks called them *planetes*, from a word of theirs meaning "wandering." The remaining stars, which did not wander but stayed put, were called "fixed stars."

Ancient astronomers were chiefly interested in the movement of the planets. Since the sun's position could be used to predict the changing of the seasons, the notion arose that the position of all the planets in combination could be used to predict all sorts of things about the future of nations, kings, and even ordinary people. This gave rise to the study of "astrology," which is still very popular today even though modern astronomers consider it nonsense.

For astrologers, the planets and the zodiac were sufficient.

TABLE 1

The Constellations of the Zodiac

(in traditional order)

LATIN NAME	PRONUNCIATION	ENGLISH NAME
Aries	AIR-eez	Ram
Taurus	TAWR-us	Bull
Gemini	GEM-ih-nigh	Twins
Cancer	KAN-ser	Crab
Leo	LEE-oh	Lion
Virgo	VUR-goh	Virgin
Libra	LIGH-bruh	Scales
Scorpius	SCOR-pee-us	Scorpion
Sagittarius	SAJ-ih-TAIR-ee-us	Archer
Capricornus	KAP-rih-KAWR-nus	Goat
Aquarius	uh-KWAIR-ee-us	Water-bearer
Pisces	PIGH-seez	Fishes

Once you start studying the stars, however, it isn't easy to stop. There are interesting star patterns outside the zodiac, and about 275 B.C. a Greek astronomer named Aratus (uh-RAY-tus) was describing and naming various constellations outside the zodiac.

His work was improved on about A.D. 135 by a Greek astronomer who lived in Egypt. His name was Claudius Ptolemaeus, but he is usually known to English-speaking people as Ptolemy (TOL-uh-mee). He listed not only twelve constellations of the zodiac, but also thirty-six constellations outside the zodiac.

Ptolemy included in each constellation only those stars that seemed to make up the picture of the animal, person, or other object for which it was named. The occasional stars that fell between such pictures Ptolemy did not include in his list of stars.

Modern astronomers couldn't allow this. Once the telescope was invented, vast numbers of stars were discovered that were too dim to be seen with the unaided eye. There were large numbers of stars between the constellations, as those were drawn in ancient times.

Astronomers today disregard the ancient pictures. Using the old constellations as a base, they divide the sky into unequal sections bounded by straight lines. Each section contains the stars of one of Ptolemy's constellations (except for a few changes when a big constellation was divided into a smaller one, or new small ones were added here and there). The constellations now cover the sky completely and there is no star that doesn't fall into one constellation or another.

Astronomers now divide the entire sky into eighty-eight constellations, and these eighty-eight constellations are listed in Table 2. The eighty-eight constellations are unevenly shaped and of different sizes. It would be neater if the sky could be divided into even sections, but it is just impossible to abandon the constellations astronomers have been using for centuries. Besides, it wouldn't do to break up the more prominent star patterns, which come in different sizes.

Most of the English names don't require any explanation (nearly half are the names of animals). A few aren't so easy and I will explain them briefly:

"Andromeda" was the name of a young woman in the Greek myths who was chained to rocks at the seashore as a sacrifice to a sea monster.

"Cassiopeia" was the name of Andromeda's mother.

"Cepheus" was the name of Andromeda's father.

The Berenice of "Berenice's Hair" was a queen of Egypt about 220 B.C.

"Hercules" was the name of the strong man of the Greek myths.

"Orion" was the name of a giant hunter in the Greek myths.

"Pegasus" was the name of the winged horse in the Greek myths.

"Perseus" was the hero in the Greek myths who rode Pegasus and rescued Andromeda.

Most important of all, as far as this book is concerned, is the "Centaur." This was a monster in Greek mythology which was pictured as having the heads, arms, and trunk of a man and the body and legs of a horse.

TABLE 2

The Constellations

LATIN NAME	PRONUNCIATION	ENGLISH NAME
Andromeda	an-DROM-uh-duh	Andromeda
Antlia	ANT-lee-uh	Air Pump
Apus	AY-pus	Bird of Paradise
Aquarius	uh-KWAIR-ee-us	Water-bearer
Aquila	AK-wih-luh	Eagle
Ara	AY-ruh	Altar
Aries	AIR-eez	Ram
Auriga	aw-RIGH-guh	Charioteer
Boötes	boh-OH-teez	Herdsman
Caelum	SEE-lum	Chisel
Camelopardalis	kuh-MEL-oh-PAHR-duh-lis	Giraffe
Cancer	KAN-ser	Crab
Canes Venatici	KAY-neez-veh-NAT-uh-sigh	Hunting Dogs
Canis Major	KAY-nis-MAY-jer	Great Dog
Canis Minor	KAY-nis-MIGH-nor	Little Dog
Capricornus	KAP-rih-KAWR-nus	Goat
Carina	kuh-RIGH-nuh	Keel
Cassiopeia	KAS-ee-oh-PEE-uh	Cassiopeia

LATIN NAME	PRONUNCIATION	ENGLISH NAME
Centaurus	sen-TAWR-us	Centaur
Cepheus	SEE-fyoos	Cepheus
Cetus	SEE-tus	Whale
Chamaeleon	kuh-MEEL-yun	Chameleon
Circinus	SUR-sih-nus	Compasses
Columba	kuh-LUM-buh	Dove
Coma Berenices	KOH-muh-BER-uh-NIGH-seez	Berenice's Hair
Corona Australis	kuh-ROH-nuh-aws-TRAY-lis	Southern Crown
Corona Borealis	Kuh-ROH-nuh-BAWR-ee-AL-is	Northern Crown
Corvus	KAWR-vus	Crow
Crater	KRAY-ter	Cup
Crux	KRUKS	Cross
Cygnus	SIG-nus	Swan
Delphinus	del-FIGH-nus	Dolphin
Dorado	duh-RAH-doh	Goldfish
Draco	DRAY-koh	Dragon
Equuleus	ih-KWOO-lee-us	Little Horse
Eridanus	ih-RID-uh-nus	River
Fornax	FAWR-naks	Furnace
Gemini	GEM-ih-nigh	Twins
Grus	GRUHS	Crane
Hercules	HUR-kyuh-leez	Hercules
Horologium	HAWR-uh-LOH-jee-um	Clock
Hydra	HIGH-druh	Snake
Hydrus	HIGH-drus	Water Snake
Indus	IN-dus	Indian
Lacerta	luh-SUR-tuh	Lizard
Leo	LEE-oh	Lion
Leo Minor	LEE-oh-MIGH-nor	Little Lion
Lepus	LEE-pus	Hare
Libra	LIGH-bruh	Scales
Lupus	LOO-pus	Wolf
Lynx	LINKS	Lynx
Lyra	LIGH-ruh	Lyre
Mensa	MEN-suh	Table
Microscopium	MIGH-kruh-SCOH-pee-um	Microscope
Monoceros	muh-NOS-uh-rus	Unicorn
Musca	MUS-kuh	Fly
Norma	NAWR-muh	Level

LATIN NAME	PRONUNCIATION	ENGLISH NAME
Octans	OK-tanz	Octant
Ophiuchus	OF-ee-YOO-kus	Serpent Holder
Orion	oh-RIGH-un	Orion
Pavo	PAY-voh	Peacock
Pegasus	PEG-uh-sus	Pegasus
Perseus	PUR-see-us	Perseus
Phoenix	FEE-niks	Phoenix
Pictor	PIK-tor	Easel
Pisces	PIGH-seez	Fishes
Piscis Austrinus	PIGH-sis-aws-TRIGH-nus	Southern Fish
Puppis	PUP-is	Stern
Pyxis	PIK-sis	Mariner's Compass
Reticulum	rih-TIK-yuh-lum	Net
Sagitta	suh-JIT-uh	Arrow
Sagittarius	SAJ-ih-TAIR-ee-us	Archer
Scorpius	SCOR-pee-us	Scorpion
Sculptor	SKULP-tor	Sculptor's Workshop
Scutum	SKYOO-tum	Shield
Serpens	SUR-penz	Serpent
Sextans	SEKS-tunz	Sextant
Taurus	TAWR-us	Bull
Telescopium	TEL-uh-SKOH-pee-um	Telescope
Triangulum	trigh-ANG-yoo-lum	Triangle
Triangulum Australe	trigh-ANG-yoo-lum-aw-STRAY-lee	Southern Triangle
Tucana	too-KAY-nuh	Toucan
Ursa Major	UR-suh-MAY-jor	Great Bear
Ursa Minor	UR-suh-MIGH-nor	Little Bear
Vela	VEE-luh	Sails
Virgo	VUR-goh	Virgin
Volans	VOH-lahnz	Flying Fish
Vulpecula	vul-PEK-yuh-luh	Little Fox

Marking off the Earth and Sky

The eighty-eight constellations recognized by astronomers today are considerably more than the forty-eight listed by Ptolemy. Some of the constellations have names Ptolemy couldn't possibly have given them. He couldn't have named "Microscopium" and "Telescopium" for he never saw or heard of microscopes and telescopes. Nor did he know of the mariner's compass, or the toucan, which is a large-billed bird native to tropical America.

The fact is that neither Ptolemy nor any of the ancient astronomers could see the whole sky, so that prior to modern times a sizable portion of the sky remained undivided into constellations. When astronomers were finally able to study, in detail, the unmarked portion of the sky, they divided it into additional constellations, sometimes with modern names.

One of the objects in the sky that could not be seen by the ancient astronomers is the subject of this book. It is therefore worth understanding why it remained hidden for so long. This is the reason:

The Earth turns about its axis from west to east, while the sky stands still. People who are on the Earth can't feel the Earth turning, however, since the motion is such a smooth one. To us on Earth, it seems that our world is standing still and that it is the sky that turns slowly (in mirror fashion, from east to west) about Earth's axis.

The Earth's axis cuts the surface of the Earth at the north pole and the south pole. If you imagine the axis extended outward till it reaches the sky, one end will reach the sky at the north celestial pole and the other will reach it at the south celestial pole. The whole sky seems to pivot slowly about the celestial poles, once every twenty-four hours.

Right in line with the Earth's equator, which is just halfway between the north and south poles, is the sky's celestial equator, which is just halfway between the north and south celestial poles. If you were standing on Earth's equator, the celestial equator would run up from the east to the zenith of the sky just over your head, and then down to the west. The north celestial pole would be right on the northern horizon, and the south celestial pole would be on the southern horizon.

The sky would seem to turn from east to west and as it turned, you could see just about all of it, with every star rising in the east, moving up and over, and setting in the west. The only part you wouldn't see would be the part behind and near the sun, but if you kept watching from day to day, the sun would slowly move and the part of the sky that had been hidden would then be seen.

Suppose you then moved northward from the equator. The bulge of the round world behind you would hide the south celestial pole, which would drop below the southern horizon. The farther north you went, the farther the south celestial pole would drop below the horizon. The north celestial pole, on the other hand, would rise in the sky as you traveled. The farther north you went, the higher the north celestial pole would be in the sky. Finally, if you reached the north pole on Earth, the north celestial pole would be directly overhead and the south celestial pole would be under your feet at the opposite end of the sky on the other side of the Earth.

It would be just the opposite if you moved southward from the equator. Then the north celestial pole would drop below the northern horizon and the south celestial pole would rise in the sky. Finally, if you reached the south pole on Earth, the south celestial pole would be directly overhead and the north celestial pole would be under your feet on the other side of the world.

(It was because this sort of thing happened as one moved north or south that the Greeks, in ancient times, began to suspect that the Earth was round and not flat.)

The position of the celestial poles in the sky is important because the stars seem to wheel about them. The celestial poles themselves do not move, but remain in one place like the hub of a turning wheel. This means that when one of the celestial poles is below the horizon, it is never seen at any time of night. It stays below the horizon forever, or at least it stays there as long as you stay in the same place on Earth.

This means that from any point north of the equator, the south celestial pole is never seen. From any point south of the equator, the north celestial pole is never seen.

Nor is it only the celestial poles themselves that are invisible. The regions in their immediate neighborhoods can also be invisible.

Suppose, for instance, that you are well north of the equator so that the position of the north celestial pole is high in the sky while the position of the south celestial pole is well below the southern horizon.

The stars in the northern part of the sky move in circles about the north celestial pole and the closer they are to the north celestial pole, the smaller and tighter is the circle they mark out in the course of the night. Particularly near the north celestial pole, the circle is so small that the stars never sink below the horizon. For that reason, stars near the north celestial pole are always visible at any time of the night to anyone standing well north of the Equator, and can be seen on any clear night of the year.

On the other hand, the stars near the south celestial pole, which is forever hidden behind the southern horizon when you stand north of the equator, move in a tight circle about it through the night. They stay so close to it that they never rise above the horizon. They are never visible from points north of the equator at any time of the night or on any night of the year.

The farther north you go, the higher the north celestial pole climbs in the sky, and the more stars in its neighborhood wheel about it without sinking below the horizon. At the same time, more and more stars in the neighborhood of the south celestial pole wheel about it and never rise above the horizon. The farther north you go, the larger the portion of the southern sky you will never see.

Finally, if you are at the north pole, the north celestial pole is directly overhead and all the stars move about in circles parallel to the horizon. All the stars above the horizon stay above the horizon and never set, but they include only the stars in the northern half of the sky. All the stars in the southern half of the sky remain below the horizon at all times and never rise—and are never seen from that spot.

Naturally, the situation is just reversed if you travel south of the equator. Then it is the south celestial pole that rises in the sky and the stars in its neighborhood that are always visible, while it is those in the neighborhood of the north celestial pole that remain below the horizon and are never visible. If you are at the south pole, the south celestial pole is directly overhead and it is the southern half of the sky you always see and the northern half you never see.

Ptolemy and all the other ancient astronomers lived and did their work well to the north of the equator, so that there was a sizable portion of the southernmost sky that they never saw and that was always and forever hidden behind the bulge of the Earth.

Exactly what parts of the sky was Ptolemy unable to see? We can answer that if we devise a method for marking off the Earth and sky in some regular way. Suppose, for instance, we draw imaginary lines around the Earth parallel to the equator, all the way from the equator to the north pole in one direction and to the south pole in the other direction. The equator itself goes all around the Earth, cutting it into two equal hemispheres. The lines parallel to the equator make progressively smaller circles.

The farther north we go, the smaller the circle we make and when we are near the north pole, the circles are very small indeed. At the north pole itself, the circles are reduced to a point. The same thing happens south of the equator, where the circles diminish to a point at the south pole.

These circles parallel to the equator are called "parallels of latitude." The word "latitude" comes from the Latin word for "wide" because on an ordinary flat map they are drawn, like the equator itself, across the width of the map. It was about 300 B.C. when a Greek geographer, Dicaearchus (DIGH-see-AHR-kus), began actually to draw east to west lines on maps.

It is customary to imagine ninety such parallels extending, at equal intervals, from the equator to the north pole, and ninety more from the equator to the south pole. The parallels are numbered as "degrees." The equator itself is at zero degrees, or 0°. As you move north you pass the one-degree parallel, the two-degree parallel and so on. Any spot on Earth that is on the one-degree mark north of the equator is said to be at "one degree north latitude." If it were on the one-degree mark south of the equator, it would be at "one degree south latitude." These can be written for short as 1° N and 1° S.

A spot on Earth could be 10° N or 25° N or 77° N, or any number of degrees up to the north pole which is 90° N. It could also be 10° S or 25° S or 77° S, all the way down to 90° S at the South Pole.

Most spots on Earth are not, of course, exactly on a parallel of latitude, but rather between parallels. Ever since ancient times it has been customary to divide the space between two degrees of latitude into sixty equal "minutes of latitude." The space between two minutes of latitude is divided into sixty equal "seconds of latitude."

A simpler method is to use decimals. A spot that is just halfway between 31° N and 32° N would be at 31.5° N. Every spot on Earth has some latitude. If you took one step northward from exactly 40° N, you would be at about 40.0000045° N.

Geographers also draw lines from the north pole to the south pole, running north and south on ordinary maps. They are called "meridians of longitude." At the equator the imaginary meridians cross one degree apart, and then there are 360 of them circling the Earth, 180 of them to the east of London, and 180 of them to the west of London. If you give the number of degrees of longitude as well as of latitude, then you can fix the precise location of any spot on Earth because there is only one spot where a particular meridian and parallel cross. (In this book, however, we won't be dealing with meridians of longitude.)

It is possible to apply the system of parallels of latitude to the sky, too. (In fact, it was applied to the sky first, because people could see that the sky was a big sphere, while they could see only a little part of the Earth and weren't sure, at first, about its shape.) There are parallels of latitude drawn from the celestial equator to each of the celestial poles, again with 90 degrees on each side. Every star can be said to be at some particular celestial latitude.

The celestial latitude is usually referred to as "declination." Instead of north and south, the signs for plus and minus are used. The equivalent of 40° N on earth is a declination of +40° in the sky, while 40° S on Earth is a declination of −40° in the sky.

By using the same system on Earth and in the sky, calculations are made simpler. If you are standing at a point on Earth that is at 40° N, then the north celestial pole is 40 degrees above the northern horizon and the south celestial pole is 40 degrees below the southern horizon. That means that any star within 40 degrees of the south celestial pole can never reach the southern horizon as it circles the pole. Such stars never rise and are therefore never seen at 40° N.

Any star that is within 40 degrees of the south celestial pole must have a declination of −50° or beyond, so that anyone standing at 40° N cannot see any star with a declination of −50° or beyond.

It works that way from any point you're standing at. If you are north of the equator and subtract 90 from your latitude, that gives you the declination marking off the stars you can't see. If you are at 20° N, you can't see any star with a declination of −70° or beyond; if you are at 65° N, you can't see any star with a declination of −25° or beyond. If you're standing at 90° N (the north pole), you can't see any part of the sky beyond 0° (the equator). You can't see the southern half of the sky at all.

It's just the reverse for the southern hemisphere. If you're standing at 20° S, you can't see any star with a declination of +70° or beyond; if you are at 65° S, you can't see any star with a declination of +25°; and if you're standing at 90° S (the south pole), you can't see any part of the sky beyond 0° (the equator). From the south pole, it is the northern half of the sky you can't see.

From the equator (at 0°) you can't see beyond +90° in one direction or beyond −90° in the other. However, +90° and −90° mark out the two celestial poles, which are the two extremes of the sky. This, therefore, is a way of saying that from the equator you can see all the stars in the sky (though some of the stars near the celestial poles are always near the horizon and can't be seen as clearly as they can be seen from other places on the Earth's surface).

The Southern Sky

Now we can get back to Ptolemy. He did his work in a city called Alexandria on the coast of Egypt. Alexandria is located at 31.1° N and from that point, Ptolemy could never see any stars with declinations beyond −58.9°. To Ptolemy, for instance, the constellation Centaurus was right on the southern horizon, where it was difficult to see.

There were, of course, people living farther south than Alexandria, even farther south than the equator. Such people could see all the way to the south celestial pole without trouble. All the ancient astronomers, however, lived north of the equator and just about all of them lived at latitudes higher than 30° N.

This situation didn't change until the Europeans began to explore the world in the 1400s. As they explored southward along the coast of Africa and, later, along the coast of South

America, they also found themselves exploring the southern sky.

In 1520, for instance, the Portuguese navigator, Ferdinand Magellan (muh-JEL-un), sailing in the service of Spain, made his way through what is now called the Strait of Magellan at the southern tip of South America. The Strait of Magellan is at 52° S, and from there the entire southern sky is visible, with the south celestial pole more than halfway to zenith.

The men sailing with Magellan noticed two dim shining patches of light high in the sky. They looked like bits torn off the Milky Way. They have been called the "Magellanic Clouds" ever since. The Large Magellanic Cloud has a declination of about −70° and the Small Magellanic Cloud about−72°. Neither is ever visible from Europe or from the United States, or from anyplace on Earth with a latitude more northerly than 20° N (which is about the latitude of Puerto Rico).

Some navigators, as they sailed southward past the equator, began to observe the southern stars carefully and to work out new constellations that Ptolemy had never seen. The first attempt came in 1595 when a Dutch navigator, Pieter Dircksz Keyser (KIGH-ser), listed twelve constellations. More were worked out by others until, by 1752, the list was complete and astronomers had the eighty-eight constellations that are listed in Table 2.

In 1930 the boundaries of all eighty-eight were made official; there is now no spot in the sky that is not part of one constellation or another. The Large Magellanic Cloud is, for instance, in Dorado, while the Small Magellanic Cloud is in Tucana.

Some of the new constellations offered particularly interesting sights. At about a declination of −60° there were to be seen four bright stars arranged so that they seemed to be at the ends of a Latin cross (just a little crooked). It may have been seen and reported first by an Italian navigator, Alvise da Cadamosto (KAH-dah-MOSE-toh), when he was exploring down the coast of Africa in 1455.

The constellation built around those four stars is Crux (Cross). It is one of the few constellations that are better known to English-speaking people by their English names, for it is commonly called "the Southern Cross."

The constellation Crux is just south of Centaurus, the constellation that Ptolemy could barely make out at the horizon sometimes. If you consider the constellation of Centaurus to be drawn as a picture of a half-human, half-horse figure (as it often is) then the horse part is usually shown toward the south while the human part is to the north. The horse's legs extend down toward the southernmost part of the constellation, and between the legs of Centaurus is the smaller constellation of Crux.

Once you got far enough south to see Crux clearly, you could also see the stars of Centaurus more clearly than ever Ptolemy could, and some of them that Ptolemy could never see at all. Cadomosto may well have seen two bright stars in the southern part of Centaurus, stars with a declination of just beyond −60° so that they were just a bit too far south for Ptolemy ever to see.

These stars are Alpha Centauri (AL-fuh-sen-TAW-righ) and Beta Centauri (BAY-tuh-sen-TAW-righ)* and it is the former that is the chief subject of this book.

---

* This pronunciation is given by Webster's. The American Heritage Dictionary gives the pronunciation as Alpha and Beta "sen-TAW-ree." I must admit I pronounce the names in the "sen-TAW-ree" fashion myself.

2
THE
STARS

The Ancient Names

The names of the particular stars mentioned at the end of the previous chapter bring us to the question of the names of stars in general. What determines the name a star will be given?

Some of the stars (not many) were given names in ancient times that were inspired by their appearance in the sky. Some of the stars with proper names are listed in Table 3, along with the pronunciation of those names and the constellation in which each is to be found.

And how were those names decided on? Here's how:

There are two bright stars only about 4 degrees apart in the sky, and they seem to be very similar in appearance. They would strike anyone as twin stars and, indeed, the constellation built around them is Gemini (the Twins). In the ancient Greek myths, there was a pair of famous twins, Castor and Pollux. It seemed natural for the Greeks to call one of the two stars Castor and the other Pollux, and we still call them by those names today.

The brightest star in the sky is named Sirius, from a Greek word meaning "glowing" or "burning," which seems appropriate for so bright a star.

Then there is a star so near the north celestial pole that it makes a very small circle about it and hardly seems to change

TABLE 3

Some Stars with Names

NAME OF STAR	PRONUNCIATION	CONSTELLATION CONTAINING IT
Achernar	AY-ker-NAHR	Eridanus
Alcor	al-KAWR	Ursa Major
Alcyone	al-SIGH-uh-nee	Taurus
Aldebaran	al-DEB-uh-ran	Taurus
Algol	AL-GOL	Perseus
Altair	al-TAH-ir	Aquila
Antares	an-TAIR-eez	Scorpius
Arcturus	ahrk-TYOOR-us	Boötes
Bellatrix	beh-LAY-triks	Orion
Betelgeuse	BEET-ul-JOOZ	Orion
Canopus	kuh-NOH-pus	Carina
Capella	kuh-PEL-uh	Auriga
Castor	KAS-ter	Gemini
Deneb	DEN-eb	Cygnus
Fomalhaut	FOH-mul-HAWT	Piscis Austrinis
Mira	MIGH-ruh	Cetus
Mizar	MIGH-ZAR	Ursa Major
Polaris	poh-LAR-is	Ursa Major
Pollux	POL-uks	Gemini
Procyon	PROH-see-ON	Canis Minor
Regulus	REG-yuh-lus	Leo
Rigel	RIGH-jul	Orion
Sirius	SIR-ee-us	Canis Major
Spica	SPIGH-kuh	Virgo
Vega	VEE-guh	Lyra

its position in the sky. It is called, in English, the North Star or the Pole Star, but its official name is Polaris, the Latin word for "polar."

In the main, though, stars received names in ancient times not from their own properties, but from their position in the images that were imagined for the various constellations. Low on the southern horizon, for instance, is the constellation of Argo, named by the Greeks for the ship that carried Jason and his Argonauts in their search for the Golden Fleece. The name of the steersman of the *Argo* was Kanopos, in Greek, and Canopus in Latin. A bright star in the constellation was named for the steersman, and since astronomers always use the Latin spelling it is named Canopus. The constellation of Argo has been broken up into smaller and more manageable groupings since ancient times, and the part with Canopus is now Carina (the "keel" of the *Argo*).

The constellation of Auriga (the Charioteer) is often pictured as a man holding the reins of a chariot in his hand and holding a goat and its kids on his lap. The goat is placed in the position of a bright star which is named Capella, a Latin word meaning "little goat."

The constellation of Virgo is often portrayed as a young woman holding a sheaf of grain. (The sun is in Virgo in early September when farmers are looking toward the harvest.) The grain is placed in the position of a bright star which is called Spica, the Latin word for an ear of grain.

The bright star, Sirius, is part of the constellation Canis Major, the Great Dog. Sirius is sometimes called the Dog Star for that reason. In the nearby constellation of Canis Minor there is another bright star, which is always in advance of Sirius as the sky turns. Because this star always rises a little before Sirius the Dog Star, it is called Procyon, from a Greek phrase meaning "before the dog."

The constellation of Boötes, the Herdsman, is located very near Ursa Major, the Great Bear. The Herdsman seems to be keeping a close eye on the Great Bear to prevent it from doing harm. A bright star in Boötes is therefore named Arcturus, from Greek words meaning "guardian of the bear."

A bright star in the constellation of Leo, the Lion, is Regulus, from the Latin word meaning "little king," an appropriate name for the star located in a constellation visualized as representing the king of beasts.

The constellation Orion, named for a giant hunter in the Greek myths, contains a number of bright stars. One is Bellatrix, which is a Latin word meaning "woman warrior." The reason for naming it that is not clear.

One star derives its name not from the constellation it is in, but from a planet. The planet Mars, which seems to shine with a reddish color reminiscent of blood, is appropriately named for the Latin god of war. The Greeks had called it by the name of *their* god of war, Ares. A star in Scorpius has a reddish appearance much like that of Mars. The Greeks therefore called it Antares, meaning "rival to Mars."

All the stars mentioned so far are among the brightest in the sky. They're the ones, naturally, which attract attention and get the names. Some dimmer ones are also named if they attract attention for some reason other than sheer brightness.

For instance, there is a little group of not very bright stars in the constellation of Taurus. No one of the group would be much noticed if it were by itself, but being in a group they attract the eye. There is no other such group in the sky that is visible to the unaided eyes (though many far more remarkable groups become visible when we look through a telescope).

The Greeks named the group of stars the Pleiades (PLEE-uh-DEEZ) after the seven daughters of the nymph Pleione (plee-OH-nee) in their myths. (Most people can make out only six stars in the group, but the seventh is there and, indeed, the telescope reveals several hundred stars that are all part of the group but that are individually too dim to see.) Each of the seven stars of the Pleiades which the ancients could make out is given the name of one of the daughters of Pleione; Alcyone is the name given to the brightest of them.

Another example of a rather dim star with a name is Mira, which is the Latin word for "wonderful." Why it should be called wonderful is because, unlike other stars, Mira varied in brightness, growing dim from time to time, then brightening again.

A surprisingly small number of stars have names that can be traced back to the ancient Greeks and Romans. Most of the stars that have names derive them from another language altogether, and one that would come as a surprise to most Westerners at first. Most of the stars have Arabic names.

During the Middle Ages, the Arabs were the important astronomers and they named many of the stars. Naturally, they named them in Arabic and many of those names have come down to us in a form that is distorted but is still recognizably that language.

A bright star in the constellation of Aquila, for instance, is named Altair, which is from Arabic words that mean simply "the star."

Many of the Arabic names describe the position of the star in the imaginary pictures suggested by the constellation. The bright star that marks the left leg of Orion is Rigel, which is the Arabic word for "leg." The star in the right shoulder of Orion is Betelgeuse, from Arabic words meaning "shoulder of the giant."

At the southern end of the curving lines of stars that make up the constellation of Eridanus (the River) is Achernar, from Arabic words meaning "end of the river." And at one end of the constellation Piscis Austrinis (the Southern Fish) is Fomalhaut, which derives its name from Arabic words meaning "mouth of the fish."

A star at one end of the constellation of Cygnus (the Swan) is Deneb, from the Arabic word for "tail." In the constellation of Taurus there is a bright star that follows right behind the Pleiades as the sky turns. It is Aldebaran, from the Arabic word for "follower." The constellation Lyra (the Lyre) was seen by the Arabs as a falling vulture, and a bright star in that constellation is Vega, from the Arabic word for "falling."

There are two stars in Ursa Major that are close together, and one of which is much dimmer than the others. The dimmer one is Alcor, from an Arabic word meaning "the weak one." The other, whose brighter light obscures the dimmer star, is Mizar from the Arabic word for "veil."

Finally, we have the star Algol in the constellation of Perseus. One of the great feats of Perseus in the Greek myths was his slaying of the Medusa, a creature with snakes for hair and with so frightful an appearance that anyone who looked at her was turned to stone. The constellation is usually drawn so as to show Perseus holding the head of Medusa, and Algol is in that head, so that it is sometimes called the "Demon Star" because of this. The meaning of Algol is not at all obscure for it is named for a particularly unpleasant demon in Arabic mythology—the "ghoul."

The Modern Names

Altogether only a few hundred stars of the six thousand that can be seen in the sky with the unaided eye have names (mostly Arabic), but even so it is almost impossible to remember those names or to know where they are in the sky. Furthermore, the stars of the southern sky, which couldn't be seen by the ancient and medieval astronomers, naturally never received names at all.

When Alpha Centauri was first sighted in the skies by European navigators it was, to them, a star without a name. Nor did anyone try to give it a simple Greek, Latin, or Arabic name to make it fit in with the longer-known stars. By that time it had begun to be recognized that some system of naming had to be worked out that would be more useful to astronomers.

The first person to try to use some logical system was a

German astronomer named Johann Bayer (BIGH-er). He published a book of star maps in 1603 and in it he introduced his system.

What he did was to name the bright stars in each constellation according to the order of their brightness or, sometimes, the order of their position. Using either system, he would list them as "the first star in the constellation Orion," "the second star in the constellation Orion," and so on—except that he made use of a more concise way of putting it.

To indicate the order, he used the letters of the Greek alphabet. For the first star he listed, he used the first letter; for the second star, he used the second letter; for the third star, the third letter, and so on. In Table 4 you will find all the letters of the Greek alphabet, some of which have become familiar to people interested in watching the stars because the names of those stars contain the letters.

According to Bayer's system, the first star in Orion would be (if the Bayer system used English) "Alpha of Orion"; the second would be "Beta of Orion" and so on.

Bayer, however, used the Latin language, and in Latin, when you want to indicate possession you don't use a preposition as English does ("of" Orion). Instead you change the ending of the word and produce what is called the "possessive form" in English, or the "genitive form" in a more nearly Latin phrase.

The genitive form of Orion is Orionis, so instead of saying "Alpha of Orion" we say "Alpha Orionis." The next stars in line are "Beta Orionis," "Gamma Orionis" and so on. Sometimes, the Greek symbol of the letter is used, so that we can write α-Orionis, β-Orionis and so on.

In Table 5 you will find a list of the genitive forms of a number of the names of the constellations (not all of them, but the ones we will have occasion to use in this book are included). Then, to give examples of the Bayer system, Table 6 repeats the stars already listed in Table 3, with names given in both fashions. The only star in Table 3 that is not in Table 6 is Alcor. There is a reason for this that we will get to shortly.

Most of the stars in Table 6 are alphas, but that's not really surprising. It was the brightest stars in each constellation that

TABLE 4

The Greek Alphabet

LETTER	PRONUNCIATION	SYMBOL
Alpha	AL-fuh	α
Beta	BAY-tuh	β
Gamma	GAM-uh	γ
Delta	DEL-tuh	δ
Epsilon	EP-sih-LON	ϵ
Zeta	ZAY-tuh	ζ
Eta	AY-tuh	η
Theta	THAY-tuh	θ
Iota	igh-OH-tuh	ι
Kappa	KAP-uh	κ
Lambda	LAM-duh	λ
Mu	MYOO	μ
Nu	NYOO	ν
Xi	ZIGH	ξ
Omicron	OM-ih-KRON	o
Pi	PIGH	π
Rho	ROH	ρ
Sigma	SIG-muh	σ
Tau	TAW	τ
Upsilon	UP-sih-LON	υ
Phi	FIGH	ϕ
Chi	KIGH	χ
Psi	SIGH	ψ
Omega	oh-MAY-guh	ω

TABLE 5

Genitive Forms of the Constellations

CONSTELLATION	GENITIVE FORM	PRONUNCIATION
Andromeda	Andromedae	an-DROM-ih-dee
Aquarius	Aquarii	uh-KWAIR-ee-igh
Aquila	Aquilae	AK-wih-lee
Aries	Arietis	uh-RIGH-uh-tis
Auriga	Aurigae	aw-RIGH-jee
Bootes	Boötis	boh-OH-tis
Cancer	Cancri	KANG-krigh
Canis Major	Canis Majoris	KAY-nis-muh-JAW-ris
Canis Minor	Canis Minoris	KAY-nis-migh-NAW-ris
Capricornus	Capricorni	KAP-rih-KAWR-nigh
Cassiopeia	Cassiopeiae	KAS-ee-oh-PEE-yee
Centaurus	Centauri	sen-TAW-righ
Cepheus	Cephei	SEE-fee-igh
Cetus	Ceti	SEE-tigh
Crux	Crucis	KROO-sis
Cygnus	Cygni	SIG-nigh
Dorado	Doradus	doh-RAH-dus
Draco	Draconis	dray-KOH-nis
Eridanus	Eridani	ee-RID-uh-nigh
Gemini	Geminorum	JEM-ih-NOH-rum
Hercules	Herculis	HUR-kyoo-lis
Hydra	Hydrae	HIGH-dree
Leo	Leonis	lee-OH-nis
Libra	Librae	LIGH-bree
Lyra	Lyrae	LIGH-ree
Ophiuchus	Ophiuchi	OHF-ee-YOO-kigh
Orion	Orionis	oh-RIGH-oh-nis
Pegasus	Pegasi	PEG-uh-sigh
Perseus	Persei	PUR-see-igh

CONSTELLATION	GENITIVE FORM	PRONUNCIATION
Pisces	Piscium	PIS-ee-um
Piscis Austrinus	Piscis Austrini	Pis-is-aws-TRIGH-nigh
Sagittarius	Sagittarii	SAJ-ih-TAIR-ee-igh
Scorpius	Scorpii	SKOR-pee-igh
Serpens	Serpentis	sur-PEN-tis
Taurus	Tauri	TAW-righ
Ursa Major	Ursae Majoris	UR-see-muh-JOH-ris
Ursa Minor	Ursae Minoris	UR-see-mih-NOR-ris
Virgo	Virginis	VUR-jih-nis

were most apt to be noticed and given names, and as Bayer frequently listed the stars in the order of their brightness, the brightest of all generally got the Alpha designation.

The Bayer system may seem unnecessarily complicated to you. Isn't it easier to say Spica than Alpha Virginis, or Polaris than Alpha Ursae Minoris?

Yes it is, but the use of the Bayer system automatically tells you where the star is. It tells you Spica is in Virgo and Polaris is in Ursa Minor. It tells you something else about them, too. It tells you each is the brightest star in the constellation.

What's more, the Bayer system can be used for dimmer stars, stars that never received any name from the Greeks, the Romans, or the Arabs. We can speak of such dim, nameless stars, important or interesting for one reason or another, as Epsilon Eridani, Tau Ceti, Chi Orionis, Zeta Doradus, or Psi Aurigae.

(In this book, however, when there are alternate names for a particular star, the one that is more familiar is always used. Thus, even though Beta Orionis is a more formal name than Rigel, the fact is that almost everyone—even astronomers— speaks of the star as Rigel every time.)

The biggest shortcoming of Bayer's system is that there are only 24 letters in the Greek alphabet and there are, on the

TABLE 6

The Bayer System

STAR	BAYER SYSTEM	
	WORDS	SYMBOLS
Achernar	Alpha Eridani	α-Eridani
Alcyone	Eta Tauri	η-Tauri
Aldebaran	Alpha Tauri	α-Tauri
Algol	Beta Persei	β-Persei
Altair	Alpha Aquilae	α-Aquilae
Antares	Alpha Scorpii	α-Scorpii
Arcturus	Alpha Boötis	α-Boötis
Bellatrix	Gamma Orionis	γ-Orionis
Betelgeuse	Alpha Orionis	α-Orionis
Canopus	Alpha Carinae	α-Carinae
Capella	Alpha Aurigae	α-Aurigae
Castor	Alpha Geminorum	α-Geminorum
Deneb	Alpha Cygni	α-Cygni
Fomalhaut	Alpha Piscis Austrini	α-Piscis Austrini
Mira	Omicron Ceti	o-Ceti
Mizar	Zeta Ursae Majoris	ζ-Ursae Majoris
Polaris	Alpha Ursae Minoris	α-Ursae Minoris
Pollux	Beta Geminorum	β-Geminorum
Procyon	Alpha Canis Minoris	α-Canis Minoris
Regulus	Alpha Leonis	α-Leonis
Rigel	Beta Orionis	β-Orionis
Sirius	Alpha Canis Majoris	α-Canis Majoris
Spica	Alpha Virginis	α-Virginis
Vega	Alpha Lyrae	α-Lyrae

average, nearly 70 visible stars per constellation. If you wanted to handle them all by the Bayer system, you would have to start using combinations of letters, and that would grow complicated.

Then, too, in 1609, only six years after Bayer established his system, the Italian scientist Galileo Galilei (GAL-ih-LAY-oh, for he is usually known by his first name only) devised a telescope which he turned on the heavens. It quickly became obvious that a far greater number of stars existed than could be seen by the unaided eye. How were they to be named?

In 1712, the English astronomer John Flamsteed turned to numbers instead. In each of the 54 constellations he could see from his observatory, he watched the stars reach the highest point in the sky (as the sky turned) and gave them numbers in the order in which they passed that highest point.

Flamsteed applied his numbering system to Cygnus, for instance, and the 61st star of that constellation to pass the highest point he called "61 Cygni." As it happens, this turned out to be an interesting star which we will mention again later in the book. Again, the star Alcor, which was so dim that Bayer never gave it a Greek-letter name (which is why it is not included in Table 6) received a number name from Flamsteed. It is "80 Ursae Majoris." Other examples of stars named in the Flamsteed fashion are "70 Ophiuchi," "107 Piscium," "61 Virginis," "55 Cancri," and "14 Herculis." Such names tell an astronomer not only the constellation in which the star is located, but even something about the location within the constellation.

Of course, as telescopes grew better, stars could be seen by the thousands in each constellation. Very dim stars came to be known by complicated systems that indicated where they could be found in certain star catalogues or by symbols indicating their exact declination. A star could be called "Lacaille 9352," for instance, where the reference is to Nicolas Louis de Lacaille (la-KAH-yuh) who prepared an important star catalogue in 1757, or "Ross 780," or "CD −46° 11,909."

Sometimes a star can be named for its discoverer, such as

"Barnard's star," named for the American astronomer Edward Emerson Barnard. While he didn't discover the star itself, he was the first to notice that it had a certain interesting property which is discussed later in the book. He reported this in 1916.

Astronomers these days use all these systems. For stars with common names, the common names are used. Where common names don't exist, bright stars are named by Bayer's system, dim stars by Flamsteed's system, and very dim stars by the catalogue system.

Now we can return to the two bright stars in the constellation of Centaurus, which Europeans first noted in the 1400s. Naturally, there was no Greek or Latin name for it since no European in ancient times had ever reported them.

Some Arabic astronomers must have been far enough south, on occasion, to see them, for the brighter one has an Arabic name. Since it appears in the leg of the Centaur, as the image of the constellation is usually drawn, they called it "Rigil Kentaurus" (RIJ-il-ken-TAW-rus) from Arabic words meaning "leg of the centaur." Frequently it is referred to as "Rigil Kent" for short. However, this name was not familiar to Europeans and it is virtually never used except in some astronomy books.

The natural tendency was to name it by the Bayer system, once that system had been invented. The brighter of the two bright stars in Centaurus was therefore named "Alpha Centauri." This is the name that is used almost universally and that is the title of this book.

The second brightest star in Centaurus is listed in some books as Agena (uh-JEE-nuh) or as Hadar (HAY-dar), but it is almost invariably referred to as Beta Centauri, as it is in this book.

The Brightest Stars

Now that we know why Alpha Centauri is called by that name, let us see how it compares with other stars.

One of the first differences you will see among the stars when you look at the sky is that some are brighter than others.

About 130 B.C. the Greek astronomer Hipparchus (hih-PAHR-kus) divided the stars into six classes of brightness, which we now refer to as "magnitudes." The brightest stars in the sky are of the "first magnitude." Somewhat dimmer stars are of the "second magnitude"; still dimmer ones of "third magnitude," then fourth and fifth, until, finally, the dimmest stars that can be seen with the unaided eyes are of "sixth magnitude."

The early astronomers counted about twenty stars as of the first magnitude. Since then, later astronomers have added a few first magnitude stars to the list, stars that early astronomers never saw. For instance, Alpha Centauri and Beta Centauri are both first magnitude stars that are on none of the ancient lists. (They are almost as close together as Castor and Pollux and, on the whole, the two bright stars of Centaurus are brighter than the two bright stars of Gemini. If the ancients had been able to see Centaurus clearly, they might have made that into the constellation of "the Twins.")

Then, too, the two brightest stars of Crux are first magnitude and they were not included on the ancient lists either since they were not seen. The two stars are Alpha Crucis and Beta Crucis. Sometimes they are called, for short, Acrux (AY-kruks) and Becrux (BEE-kruks) but these are not familiar names and this book will use the Bayer names for them.

In Table 7 you will find the twenty-two stars that are now considered to be the first-magnitude stars of the sky. They are listed in order of declination from north to south.

The first-magnitude stars are spread around the sky fairly evenly. From the north pole you could see the eleven with positive declinations, and from the south pole you could see the eleven with negative declination. From a point on the equator, of course, you could see them all.

The most northerly first-magnitude star, Capella, has a declination of $+46.0°$, so it can be seen from any point north of $44°$ S. The only inhabited land area lying south of $44°$ S is the extreme southern tip of South America. The most southerly

TABLE 7

First-Magnitude Stars, by Declination

STAR	DECLINATION (DEGREES)
Capella	+46.0
Deneb	+45.1
Vega	+38.7
Castor	+32.0
Pollux	+28.2
Arcturus	+19.5
Aldebaran	+16.4
Regulus	+12.2
Altair	+ 8.7
Betelgeuse	+ 7.4
Procyon	+ 5.4
Rigel	− 8.3
Spica	−10.9
Sirius	−16.7
Antares	−26.3
Fomalhaut	−29.9
Canopus	−52.7
Achernar	−57.5
Beta Crucis	−59.4
Beta Centauri	−60.1
Alpha Centauri	**−60.6**
Alpha Crucis	−62.8

first-magnitude star, Alpha Crucis, has a declination of −62.8°, so it can be seen only from points farther south than 27.2° N, which means it cannot be seen from any point farther north than Miami, Florida.

This means that from the inhabited land in the Tropic Zone

and in the South Temperate Zone we can see all twenty-two first-magnitude stars in the sky. It is only in the North Temperate Zone that we begin missing some. From any place north of Richmond, Virginia, or any place north of the Mediterranean Sea, the five southernmost first-magnitude stars cannot be seen—and that includes Alpha Centauri.

Notice that the twenty-two first-magnitude stars are from eighteen different constellations—another sign of how well they are spread over the sky. Four constellations: Gemini, Orion, Crux, and Centaurus have two first-magnitude stars each; fourteen others have one each. That leaves seventy constellations with no first-magnitude stars.

This doesn't mean that constellations without first-magnitude stars may not be spectacular just the same. Ursa Major, without a single first-magnitude star and with not one star that is commonly known by name, has seven stars arranged as a large and very noticeable "Big Dipper." Six of these stars are second-magnitude and one is third-magnitude, and it is probably the most easily recognized star combination in the sky.

Again, the constellation of Cassiopeia, without any first-magnitude stars, has three second-magnitude stars and two third-magnitude stars arranged in a very noticeable W-shape.

The most famous star of all, perhaps, is Polaris, which is located at a declination of $+89.0°$, just one degree from the north celestial pole. It is so close to the north celestial pole and makes so tight a circle about it that it hardly appears to move in the sky. As a way of determining which direction is north, uncounted millions of eyes have sought it out—yet it is only second-magnitude.

Polaris also serves to mark out (approximately) the site of the north celestial pole, which is just an imaginary spot in the sky. (The south celestial pole does not have any star brighter than the fifth magnitude within several degrees of itself.)

So, although this book tends to concentrate on the first-magnitude stars, because Alpha Centauri is one of them, please remember that they don't represent the whole of the sky by any means.

The Tenth-Brightest Object

Of course, the early astronomers had to judge the brightness of stars by eye and that isn't easy to do. That was probably why Bayer got a few of his alphas and betas backward. It was also why, faced with a group of stars of approximately equal brightness, as in the case of the stars of the Big Dipper, he made no decision, but just listed them from one side to the other in order, beginning with Alpha and ending with Zeta.

In the 1800s, though, astronomers using telescopes and other instruments for the purpose were able to compare the brightness of stars very accurately. It turned out that some of the first-magnitude stars were considerably brighter than other first-magnitude stars. It also turned out that the average first-magnitude star was about a hundred times as bright as the average sixth-magnitude star.

In 1850 an English astronomer, Norman Robert Pogson (POG-sun), suggested that magnitudes be made more exact. If the average first-magnitude star is one hundred times as bright as the average sixth-magnitude star, and if we go down the magnitude list in five equal steps (1 to 2; 2 to 3; 3 to 4; 4 to 5; and 5 to 6) then we can suppose that a star of one magnitude is 2.512 times as bright as the star of the next dimmer magnitude. This is because five 2.512's multiplied together ($2.512 \times 2.512 \times 2.512 \times 2.512 \times 2.512$) are equal to just about 100.

One can also calculate how much of a change in brightness is equal to a tenth of a magnitude and even a hundredth of a magnitude. Then, if the first-magnitude average is set equal to 1.00, one can measure the brightness of each star and find some particular star to have a magnitude of 1.78, another 3.91 or 5.09, and so on.

Since the value of 1.00 is taken as the average for the first-magnitude stars, those brighter than average must have a magnitude of less than 1. A brighter-than-average first-magnitude star may have a magnitude of 0.59 for instance. If a star is particularly bright, the magnitude may be even less than zero, forcing astronomers to go into the negative numbers.

The thing to remember is that the lower the numerical value of the magnitude, the brighter the star, and that a negative magnitude is a matter of brightness indeed. Only four stars are so bright that they must be listed as having negative magnitudes. In Table 8, the twenty-two first-magnitude stars are listed in the order of brightness.

Since four of the constellations have two first-magnitude stars, four of the stars in Table 8 are Betas: Beta Orionis (Rigel), Beta Geminorum (Pollux), Beta Centauri, and Beta Crucis. The last two are dimmer than Alpha Centauri and Alpha Crucis respectively, but the first two are oddly misnamed. Beta Orionis (Rigel) is brighter than Alpha Orionis (Betelgeuse); and Beta Geminorum (Pollux) is brighter than Alpha Geminorum (Castor). Bayer, working by eye, probably didn't try to distinguish the brighter from the dimmer in the case of Orion and Gemini and got them wrong.

Some stars that almost make the list of first-magnitude stars should be mentioned. The third-brightest star of Crux, "Gamma Crucis," has a magnitude of 1.61, which is barely short of the first-magnitude level. Of the four stars of the Southern Cross, two are first-magnitude and a third is nearly first-magnitude. Combining these with the quite close pair of stars Alpha Centauri and Beta Centauri, which are not far from the Southern Cross, you have a collection of five stars not matched anywhere else in the sky for brilliance—and northerners do not see it.

Again, Bellatrix, the third brightest star of Orion, has a magnitude of 1.70 not far from first-magnitude. A little brighter, and it would give Orion three first-magnitude stars (though not as closely spaced as the three in Crux).

TABLE 8

First-Magnitude Stars, by Brightness

STAR	MAGNITUDE
Sirius	—1.42
Canopus	—0.72
Alpha Centauri	**—0.27**
Arcturus	—0.06
Vega	0.04
Capella	0.05
Rigel	0.14
Procyon	0.38
Achernar	0.51
Beta Centauri	0.63
Altair	0.77
Betelgeuse	0.80
Aldebaran	0.86
Alpha Crucis	0.90
Spica	0.91
Antares	0.92
Pollux	1.16
Fomalhaut	1.19
Deneb	1.26
Beta Crucis	1.28
Regulus	1.36
Castor	1.58

The brightest star of the Big Dipper, Alioth (AL-ee-oth, from an Arabic word meaning "tail of a sheep" because it is in the tail of the Great Bear as it is usually drawn), has a magnitude of 1.68, again not far from first-magnitude level.

The magnitude of Polaris is 2.12 and of Mizar 2.16. Alcyone, the brightest star of the Pleiades, has a magnitude of 3.0, while the dimmer stars of the group are about 5.4. Alcor has a magnitude of 4.0.

Let us, however, return to Alpha Centauri. You see from Table 8 that it is the third-brightest star in the sky. Only Canopus and Sirius outshine it. Canopus has a lower magnitude by 0.45, which means that it is one and a half times as bright as Alpha Centauri. Sirius, which is by far the brightest star in the sky, is 1.15 magnitudes lower than Alpha Centauri, which means that it is about three times as bright as Alpha Centauri and twice as bright as the second-brightest star.

Yet there are objects in the sky that are brighter than even the brightest stars. The planets, unlike most stars, tend to change brightness as they circle the sky. When at their brightest, however, each planet known to the ancients is brighter than Alpha Centauri. And so, of course, are the moon and the sun.

TABLE 9

The Brightest Objects in the Sky

OBJECT	NATURE	MAGNITUDE (AT BRIGHTEST)	BRIGHTNESS (ALPHA CENTAURI = 1)
Alpha Centauri	Star	—0.27	1
Saturn	Planet	—0.4	1.13
Canopus	Star	—0.72	1.5
Mercury	Planet	—1.2	2.5
Sirius	Star	—1.42	2.9
Jupiter	Planet	—2.5	7.1
Mars	Planet	—2.8	10
Venus	Planet	—4.3	40
Moon	Satellite	—12.6	83,000
Sun	Sun	—26.9	44,000,000,000

Some comets also have a total brightness greater than that of Alpha Centauri, but comets are so different from other celestial objects visible to the unaided eye, and come and go so irregularly, that they are better left out of consideration when it comes to comparisons. Then, too, there is the very occasional case of a dim star which explodes and becomes extraordinarily bright, much brighter than Alpha Centauri, for a short period of time. Those, too, are exceptional cases, and can be omitted from considerations.

If we confine ourselves to normal objects always present in the sky, we can prepare Table 9 in which all those brighter than Alpha Centauri are listed. As you can see, of the normal inhabitants of Earth's sky, Alpha Centauri turns out to be the tenth-brightest.

3

THE
PROBLEM
OF
DISTANCE

Proper Motion

But why the difference in the magnitudes of the stars? The general opinion, in early times, was that all the stars were at the same distance from the Earth; that they were all part of the sky ("the celestial sphere") which was a solid sphere enclosing the Earth, moon, sun, and planets. No one knew just how far the sky was from the Earth, but that didn't affect the argument. What was also thought was that the stars were different in size and that the larger ones were brighter than the smaller ones. In fact, the word "magnitude" means "size."

The reason the planets were brighter than the stars, people had thought since early times, was that the planets were nearer Earth than the starry sky was. Furthermore, the planets differed in brightness among themselves, and it might be thought that the nearer a planet was, the brighter it was.

The ancients judged the distance of the planets by the speed with which they moved among the stars. The more rapidly they moved, the closer to us they must be. (Thus, we know in our own experience, an airplane moving overhead rather close to us seems to zoom past at a great rate while another airplane, a great distance overhead, seems to move slowly across the sky, even though it may be moving more rapidly, in actual fact, than the nearby plane. We notice the slowing in apparent motion as distance increases with automobiles, with people, and with everything on Earth, so why not with the planets in the heavens?)

Judging by the speed of motion, the ancients judged the planetary system to be arranged in the following manner, in the order of increasing distance from Earth: Moon, Mercury, Venus, Sun, Mars, Jupiter, and Saturn.

The sun is incomparably the brightest even though there are three objects closer, and it is clearly larger than any of the other objects. Only the moon rivals it in apparent size, but then it is so much closer than the sun is. Again, Venus is brighter than Mercury, though farther away, and Jupiter is brighter than Mars though farther away. Venus must therefore be larger than Mercury and Jupiter larger than Mars, and the conclusion is that with planets, both size and distance contribute to differences in magnitude.

To be sure, once it was understood that the sun and not the Earth was the center of the planetary system, it became apparent that rapidity of motion was not a sure guide to distance, because the motion was about the sun and therefore gave a notion as to the distance from the sun rather than from the Earth. By modern notions, the order of distance from Earth is: Moon, Venus, Mars, Mercury, Sun, Jupiter, and Saturn. That does not affect the conclusion, however, since Jupiter is still brighter than Mars.

In the 1600s, after the telescope was invented, it quickly became apparent that the planets shone only by reflected light from the sun. The closer they were to the sun, the more light they received and reflected. The larger they were, the more light they received and reflected. By the end of the 1600s both the distances and the sizes of the planets were determined and the original notion that their magnitudes depended on both distance and size was confirmed.

Well, then, what about the stars?

The planets increase in size when looked at through the

telescope and seem like little circles, ellipses, crescents, and so on. The stars, however, do not. They become brighter when viewed through the telescope, but are still so small that they seem only points of light. From this, it would seem that the stars are much more distant from us than the planets are and are therefore such small objects that even telescopic magnification doesn't make them large enough to make them seem like more than points.

If that is the case, it does not seem likely that the stars, like the planets, shine by reflected light from the sun. At the much greater distance of the stars, they would not catch enough light from the sun to be visible. Therefore they must shine by their own light. The only heavenly body we know that certainly shines by its own light is the sun. Can it be, then, that the stars are other suns that look like tiny points of light only because they are so distant?

Actually, as long ago as 1440 a German scholar, Nicholas of Cusa (KYOO-suh), had suggested that stars were distant suns, but in his time that was only a guess. He had no evidence.

Of course, even though the stars were other suns and very far away, they might still be all at the same great distance, and differences in brightness might still be the result of differences in size only.

The first astronomer who made a discovery that indicated something else to be true was the Englishman Edmund Halley (HAL-ee). He was carefully making note of the positions of the stars, and in 1718 he announced that he had discovered that the stars Sirius, Procyon, and Arcturus had changed their positions with reference to their neighbors since the ancient Greeks had reported those positions. They had even changed their positions slightly from those reported a century and a half earlier.

Apparently the stars were not fixed in space as the early astronomers had thought. They had "proper motions." (The motion is "proper" because it belongs to the star itself and not to the sky that earlier had seemed to turn and carry all the stars along with it.)

But not every star has a proper motion, at least one that is large enough to measure. The first proper motions to be noted were those of bright stars. Sirius is the brightest star in the sky, Arcturus the fourth-brightest and Procyon the eighth-brightest.

Suppose that the stars all moved, but that the rate at which they moved depended (as in the case of the planets) on how close they were to us. Since stars were so far away they would all be moving very, very slowly, and the change in their position would become noticeable only after the lapse of years of time. The change would become noticeable more quickly, however, in the case of stars closer to us, and in the ones that were closest of all, the change would become most noticeable.

Surely it could not be coincidence that the first stars whose proper motion was noticed were bright ones. In fact, all the bright stars had a proper motion (though some moved more rapidly than others). Dim stars, on the other hand, which made up the majority of the stars in the sky, had very slight proper motions and most of them had proper motions so slight they could not be measured at all. (That meant that dim stars could be used as fixed reference points against which to measure the proper motion of the brighter stars.)

Since the bright stars had noticeable proper motions and might therefore be assumed to be closer than dim stars, it might also be that they were bright *because* they were close. It might be that instead of stars all being at the same distance, and differing in magnitude because they differed in size, they were all the same size but differed in magnitude because they differed in distance.

Of course, even proper motions that are large enough to be measured aren't very great. (Nor would you expect them to be if the stars were very much more distant than the planets, as seemed certain.) Proper motions are so small that even the greatest of them represent a shift in position of a star in the course of a year that can be measured only in terms of seconds of arc. And remember that one second of arc is 1/60 of a minute of arc, which is in turn 1/60 of a degree.

To give you a notion of how large a second of arc is, the width of the full moon is 1865 seconds of arc, or 1865", on the average. (The width changes slightly, because the moon does not go around Earth in a perfect circle and is a little closer to us in some positions in its orbit than in other positions.) One second of arc is therefore 1/1865 the average width of the full moon.

The proper motion of Sirius is 1.324" per year, which means that it will take Sirius 1400 years to shift position in the sky by an amount equal to the full moon. This is a very slow movement indeed, but between the time the Greeks had recorded the position of Sirius and the time Halley did, 1700 years had passed and the shift was about 2250" or about ⅝ of a degree. That kind of shift would be noticed even with the unaided eye, let alone a telescope.

In Table 10 the proper motions are given for the twenty brightest stars in the sky, in decreasing order of size.

The Fastest Stars

As you can see from Table 10, of the bright stars, the second, third, and fourth most rapidly moving are Arcturus, Sirius, and Procyon respectively—and these are precisely the ones whose proper motion Halley first noted. Why did he not note the one that is in first place, Alpha Centauri? Because Alpha Centauri is located so far to the south on the celestial sphere that the Greeks had made no observations of its position which Halley could then compare to modern observations.

Later observations soon revealed Alpha Centauri's motion, however, for it shifted position so quickly that its motion could be detected in very little time. Alpha Centauri's proper

TABLE 10

The Proper Motion of the Brightest Stars

STAR	PROPER MOTION (SECONDS OF ARC)	NUMBER OF YEARS TO SHIFT THE WIDTH OF THE MOON
Alpha Centauri	**3.682**	**506**
Arcturus	2.287	815
Sirius	1.324	1,410
Procyon	1.242	1,500
Altair	0.659	2,830
Pollux	0.623	2,990
Capella	0.437	4,270
Fomalhaut	0.367	5,080
Vega	0.348	5,360
Aldebaran	0.205	9,100
Achernar	0.093	20,100
Beta Crucis	0.054	34,500
Spica	0.051	36,600
Alpha Crucis	0.048	38,900
Beta Centauri	0.039	47,800
Betelgeuse	0.032	58,300
Antares	0.032	58,300
Canopus	0.022	84,800
Deneb	0.004	466,000
Rigel	0.003	622,000

motion is the highest by far among the bright stars; it is 1.7 times as high as that of Sirius, which is in second place. If the amount of proper motion is an indication of the closeness of a star, it would seem that Alpha Centauri may be the nearest of the bright stars. Then, if brightness is itself an indication of closeness, and if no dim star can possibly be as close to us as a bright star is, it might be that Alpha Centauri is the nearest of all the stars.

But wait! It is not a safe assumption that any dim star must be farther away than any bright star.

Once astronomers were alerted to the existence of proper motion, they began to compare the positions of all stars to those recorded by the Greeks. They also began to compare the positions of dim stars (which the Greeks did not see, or if they did, did not bother to pinpoint) from year to year. They found that, indeed, almost all dim stars had no detectable proper motion, but that *some* dim stars, even some very dim stars, had considerable proper motion.

The first astronomer to make a wholesale attempt to measure proper motions was an Italian, Giuseppi Piazzi (PYAH-tsee). He not only showed that bright stars generally had detectable proper motions, but in 1814 he reported that the dim star 61 Cygni, which was only of the fifth magnitude, had a rapid proper motion, one that was nearly half again that of Alpha Centauri.

And in 1916 Edward Emerson Barnard noted the still more rapid proper motion of a star still dimmer than 61 Cygni, a star in fact that was of the ninth magnitude and was far too dim to see without a telescope. Yet, despite its dimness, its proper motion was nearly twice that of 61 Cygni and nearly three times that of Alpha Centauri. Although many had noted the star before, it was Barnard who first pointed out its proper motion and it is therefore called "Barnard's star" in his honor.

So rapid is the motion of Barnard's star that it is sometimes called "Barnard's runaway star" or "Barnard's arrow." Its proper motion is such that it will take 181 years to shift its position as much as the width of the moon, which is very slow by earthly standards, but very fast indeed by stellar standards.

Among the bright stars, only Alpha Centauri has a proper

motion of more than 3″ per year. If we include dim stars as well, however, we find a sizable number exceeding that mark. In Table 11, the stars with a proper motion of more than 3″ per year are listed.

Of the twenty-one stars listed in Table 11, only one, Alpha Centauri, is a first-magnitude star. Five more are dim stars, fourth- and fifth-magnitude, and have names according to the Bayer or Flamsteed system. They are, in decreasing order of brightness: Phi Eridani, Omicron Eridani, Epsilon Indi, 61 Cygni, and Mu Cassiopeiae. The remaining fifteen stars are so dim that only a telescope will reveal them, and they are named after the astronomer who first noted their proper motion (or some other interesting fact about them), or by their listing in a catalogue, or some other way.

Barnard's star, even six decades after the discovery of its proper motion, remains the fastest-moving star known. It doesn't seem likely that anything faster-moving has managed to escape astronomical notice in all this time, but stranger things have happened, and if something yet faster remains to be found, it could be something very exciting indeed, as we shall see later.

If we judge by proper motion alone, then we should decide that Barnard's star is closer to us than Alpha Centauri, but then why should Barnard's star be so dim and Alpha Centauri, the more distant, so bright? Alpha Centauri, though farther away, if we judge by proper motion, is 10,000 times as bright as Barnard's star. The easiest conclusion is that Barnard's star, though very close, is a very small and very dim star, whose feeble flicker can barely be picked up in the telescope even though it is so close.

By this we can see that brightness alone is no criterion of distance. On the average, bright stars are closer to us than dim stars are, but a given dim star might be dim chiefly because of its small size, and might be closer than a given bright star.

TABLE 11

The Proper Motion of the Fastest Stars

STAR	MAGNITUDE	PROPER MOTION (SECONDS OF ARC)	NUMBER OF YEARS TO SHIFT THE WIDTH OF THE MOON
Barnard's Star	9.67	10.30	181
Kapteyn's Star	8.8	8.76	213
Groombridge 1830	6.46	7.05	265
Cordoba 31353	7.44	6.90	270
Lacaille 9352	7.2	6.87	271
Cordoba 32416	8.3	6.11	305
Ross 619	12.5	5.40	345
61 Cygni	5.12	5.27	354
22H Camelopardis	7.60	4.78	390
Epsilon Indi	4.74	4.70	397
BO 7899	8.9	4.52	413
Wolf 359	13.5	4.48	416
Omicron Eridani	4.48	4.08	457
Wolf 489	13	3.94	473
Mu Cassiopeiae	5.26	3.76	496
Alpha Centauri	**—0.27**	**3.682**	**506**
OAs 14320	9.9	3.68	507
Luyten 726-8	12.5	3.35	557
Luyten 789-6	12.2	3.27	570
Phi Eridani	4.30	3.16	590
Van Maanen's Star	12.34	3.01	620

Furthermore, we can't judge by proper motion alone either. After all, we don't really know that all stars are moving at the same real speed. Whatever the speed in reality, very distant stars will seem to be moving more slowly than very close stars. On the other hand, if two stars are nearly at the same distance, the difference in proper motion may be the result of differences in real motion rather than of distance.

For instance, it may be that Barnard's star just happens to be moving ten times as quickly as Alpha Centauri. In that case Barnard's star will have a larger proper motion than Alpha Centauri, even though Barnard's star may be somewhat the farther of the two.

Then again, much depends on the direction of the star's motion. After all, the proper motion that we see represents only the motion at right angles to us. Suppose that two stars are moving at the same speed, but that one is moving directly toward us or directly away from us, and the other is moving directly across our line of vision. The star moving directly toward us or away from us would not change its position compared with other stars, no matter how fast it was moving. It would seem to have no proper motion. The star moving directly across our line of vision would show a proper motion, perhaps even a large one, even though it was moving no faster than the star with no proper motion. If a star were moving at a slant, only that part of the slant that would be across our line of vision would show up as proper motion.

It might then be that Barnard's star might be moving rather slowly but in a direction directly across our line of vision, while Alpha Centauri was moving more rapidly, but in a direction nearly toward us or away from us. In that case, Alpha Centauri might seem to have a smaller proper motion even if it were closer to us than Barnard's star is.

In fact, neither brightness nor proper motion, nor both in combination, can tell us how far away a particular star is— or even whether one particular star is nearer or farther than another star. All we can say is that bright stars are nearer us than dim stars *on the average,* and that fast-moving stars are nearer us than slow-moving stars *on the average.*

We need something better than that.

Parallax

To determine the distance of something we can't reach, we can make use of something called "parallax" from Greek words meaning "change of position." The system is not a modern one; it was known to the ancient Greeks.

You can see how this works if you hold a finger out in front of your eyes at arm's length. If you close one eye, you will see the finger against some object in the background. If you hold your finger steady and close the other eye, you will see its apparent position against the background shift.

If you bring the finger closer to yourself you will see that the change in position as you use first one eye and then the other becomes greater. By measuring the amount of the change in position you can determine the distance of your finger from your eye.

By using your eyes one at a time, you cannot measure very great distances; only those of several feet at most. For objects too far away the change in position is so small you can't measure it accurately. But then, the shift depends not only on distance but on the separation of the two points from which the object is viewed. Your eyes are separated by only a few inches and that isn't much of a "base line."

Suppose you planted two stakes six feet apart. If you viewed an object first from one stake, then from the other, you would increase the amount of the parallax for a given distance and an object could then be much farther away before the parallax became too small to measure.

Your base line might be greater than six feet, too—much greater.

Suppose the moon is observed at a particular time through a telescope placed at a certain position on Earth's surface. The moon is then seen in some particular position against the background of stars. If it is observed at the same time through a telescope in another observatory, it will seem to be in a somewhat different position. From the exact amount of the change in the position in fractions of a degree, and from the exact distance between the two telescopes, the distance of the moon can be calculated by the branch of mathematics known as trigonometry.

In the case of the moon, the parallax, though not very large, is still large enough to measure not only with a telescope, but even with the unaided eye. That means that even ancient astronomers could measure it and get a fairly good idea of the distance of the moon. Modern astronomers have, of course, managed to use the technique more precisely and it turns out that the average distance of the moon from Earth is 384,400 kilometers (238,900 miles).

This is a great distance by earthly standards (it is twenty-five times the airline distance from New York to Melbourne, Australia) but it is very small compared to the distance of other heavenly bodies. No other heavenly body but the moon has a parallax large enough to be measured without a telescope. (A telescope magnifies tiny changes in position and makes it possible to measure them.)

It wasn't till near the end of the 1600s, after the invention of the telescope, that the parallax of Mars, which is much more distant than the moon and therefore has a much smaller parallax, could be measured. Once that was done, its distance and the distances between other bodies in the solar system could be determined.

The distance of Earth from the sun, for instance, is now known to be 150,000,000 kilometers (93,000,000 miles), which is 390 times the distance from Earth to the moon.

The farthest known planet prior to 1781 was Saturn, and its average distance from the sun is 1,425,000,000 kilometers (886,000,000 miles). The farthest known planet today is Pluto, and its average distance from the sun is 5,900,000,000 kilometers (3,666,000,000 miles).

Suppose we consider the width of the solar system as the distance across the orbit of Pluto. That comes to 11,800,000,000 kilometers (7,300,000,000 miles).

Distances in the billions of kilometers are hard to grasp,

but then the kilometer (or the mile) is a unit of measure made for the convenience of earthly distances. It would be easier to take the distance of Earth from the sun as a unit with which to measure distances in the solar system. In fact, the distance of Earth from the sun is called an "astronomical unit" (A.U.).

Since the distance of Saturn from the sun is, on the average, 9.53 times as great as the distance of Earth from the sun, Saturn is 9.53 A.U. from the sun. In the same way, the orbit of Pluto has a width of 79 A.U.

It might seem, though, that the usefulness of parallax is confined to the solar system itself. If observatories are placed as far apart as possible on the Earth's surface, the moon's parallax is about 2°. The parallax of Mars, however, only about 30" at most, is only 1/240th the parallax of the moon. The parallax of Mars, though too small to measure with the unaided eye, can easily be measured by telescope and from that, all other distances in the solar system can be calculated.

But what about the stars? Even the closest stars must be so much farther than Mars that from even the most separated observatories on Earth's surface, the parallax must be so tiny that no telescope we have built or are likely to build in the foreseeable future could measure it.

Are we sure? Can we really be so pessimistic if we don't know what the distance of the stars is to begin with? Is there any way of at least getting some notion of the distance without using parallax?

The first person to attempt to do this in a logical way was Halley, the astronomer who had been the first to detect proper motion. Having realized that the stars were moving about independently and that they might be distant suns, he asked himself this: Suppose Sirius were really as bright as the sun; how far away must it be to appear as a spark of light no brighter than it is?

The brightness of an object like the sun would decrease with distance according to a formula that was well known even in Halley's time, so the problem could be easily solved. Halley decided that Sirius would have to be about 19,000,000,000,000 kilometers (11,600,000,000,000 miles) away. Such a distance is enormous, thousands of times the distances within the solar system. The distance of Sirius by Halley's calculations would be over 21,000 times as great as the distance of Saturn, the farthest-known planet in his time. It would be 1,600 times the width of Pluto's orbit.

The distance of Sirius, by Halley's calculation, is so large that using astronomical units to express it isn't very helpful. By his calculation, Sirius is about 204,000 A.U. away.

Is there some more reasonable unit we could use? Astronomers today make use of the speed of light for the purpose. The first reasonable determination of the speed of light came in 1676, thanks to the work of a Danish astronomer, Olaus Roemer (ROY-mur). His original measurement wasn't very accurate but it has been greatly improved in the three centuries since, and at the present time we know that in one second a ray of light, moving through a vacuum, will travel 299,792.4562 kilometers (186,282.3959 miles). We will be close enough if we say that the speed of light is about 300,000 kilometers per second (186,300 miles per second).

The speed of light is much faster than any of the speeds with which we are acquainted. We think a plane is moving rapidly if it goes 3,000 kilometers an hour, or a rocket if it is going 60,000 kilometers an hour, or Earth, because it travels about the sun at the rate of 107,000 kilometers an hour—but even the Earth is moving at only 1/100,000 the speed of light.

The fact is that no material object can travel faster than light. Light travels at the speed limit for our universe. That means we can scarcely do better than to use light to measure great distances.

So fast is light that it will travel from here to the moon in about 1.25 seconds, from here to the sun in 8.3 minutes, and across the full width of the solar system in eleven hours.

But imagine light traveling at its enormous speed for a whole year. What distance will it cover? The answer is 9,460,-600,000,000 kilometers (5,878,500,000,000 miles). That distance is therefore called a "light-year." Sirius, by Halley's calculations, would therefore be two light-years away.

Of course, this figure would depend on whether Sirius was really as bright as the sun, as Halley assumed. If it were less bright than the sun, it would have to be closer than two light-years to be as bright as it appears, and if it were brighter than the sun, it would have to be farther.

Even if we recognize the fact that Sirius may not be as bright as the sun, and that Halley didn't have a very accurate notion of how far the sun was from the Earth to begin with, so that his calculations might be off by quite a bit, it seems fair to assume that even the nearest stars are at light-year distances. In that case, the parallax of the stars, when viewed from different observatories on Earth's surface, could not possibly be more than 1/10,000 of a second of arc—far too small to measure.

On the other hand, the Earth moves about the sun in an orbit the full width of which is 300,000,000 kilometers (186,-000,000 miles), more than 23,000 times the width of the Earth. If a star were observed at some particular time and then again six months later, it would be seen from two places separated by 23,000 times the width of the Earth. With such a hugely enlarged base line, the parallax for an object at a particular distance would be correspondingly enlarged.

Even that did not make the problem simple. The enlarged parallax would not be more than a second of arc or so at best, for objects at light-year distances. This change might be obscured by the larger shift in position caused by proper motion or by some other tiny position shifts of the stars for reasons that have nothing to do with parallax.

More than a century passed after Halley's estimate and even

as the 1830s opened, astronomers had been unable to measure the parallax of any star (or the "stellar parallax" as it was called, from the Latin word for "star").

Double Stars

One important attempt to determine the distance of the nearer stars failed, but produced important results in connection with the notion of "double stars."

Anyone looking at the stars with the unaided eye sees them as individual sparks of light, which are not evenly spread over the sky. Some stars happen to be located fairly close to each other, and when that happens, they generally attract attention. The Pleiades are a case of six or seven rather dim stars close together. Another case is that of Mizar and Alcor.

Mizar and Alcor were the best-known example of a double star known to the ancients who had only their eyes to use. One point of interest lay in the difference in brightness of the two stars. Mizar's magnitude of 2.2 makes it five times as bright as Alcor, which has a magnitude of 4.0.

Mizar's brightness tends to wash out nearby Alcor and make it hard to see. Indeed, some ancients used the two stars as a test of good eyesight, for it took keen vision to make out the dimmer star in the glare of the brighter one.

Mizar and Alcor could by no means remain the most remarkable example of double stars once astronomers began to use telescopes. Since the telescope reveals many more stars than can be seen by the naked eye, these stars must be closer together on the average and there must be many cases of double stars. Indeed, it would seem inevitable that the telescope would reveal pairs of dim stars so close together that they would seem like one star if they could be viewed by the unaided eye.

Then, too, bright well-known stars that *were* seen as individual sparks of light turned out to be very closely spaced stars when viewed in the telescope.

The first case of this was discovered in 1650 by the Italian astronomer Giovanni Battista Riccioli (ree-CHOH-lee). Observing Mizar through his telescope, he found that it was made up of two stars only a few seconds of arc apart. (At the moment, they are 14.3″ apart.) No human eye without a telescope could possibly distinguish two stars so close together. Mizar is not only a "visual double star" thanks to its nearness to Alcor; it is also a "telescopic double star," the first to be discovered.

Other examples of this were found, and by 1784 catalogues were prepared containing eighty-nine examples of such telescopic double stars. Included in the list was Alpha Centauri, which Lacaille had discovered in the 1750s to be a double star, with the two stars less than 22″ apart.

It has become customary to name the two stars of a telescopic star "A" and "B," with A reserved for the brighter of the two. Thus, the star we refer to as Alpha Centauri is actually Alpha Centauri A and Alpha Centauri B.

By then, though, the discovery of proper motion made it plain that stars were at different distances. For that reason, it was clear that closeness against the background of the sky did not necessarily mean closeness in actual fact. Astronomers decided that what seemed to be double stars were really single stars that were far apart, but that just happened to lie in the same direction when viewed from Earth. Whichever one of the double stars was dimmer was assumed to be the farther away of the two.

If that were the case, a double star offered a convenient way of measuring stellar parallax. The dimmer of the pair was bound to be so far away that its parallax would have to be too small to be detected even by use of Earth's great sweep about the sun. It could therefore be considered as fixed in position and as a motionless reference for the other star which was brighter, and therefore closer, and therefore might display a tiny parallax.

Why not, then, observe a double star month after month,

measuring the small distance between the two stars and noting how they might change very slightly. If the brighter star showed a parallax, the distance would change in a very definite way in the course of a year. There would be no mistaking it.

In the 1780s, this task was undertaken by the German-English astronomer William Herschel (HUR-shel). He scoured the sky for useful double stars and was entirely too successful. It began to seem to him that there were too many of them.

If the number of stars that existed down to a certain magnitude of brightness were distributed across the sky in a random way, there would be a certain chance that a particular pair of stars would be quite close together; a certain smaller chance that they would be even closer together and so on. The way of calculating such things was well known and it turned out that the number of double stars was far greater than chance would account for.

It might be, then, that stars weren't distributed in a random way after all; that stars might sometimes belong together. Herschel studied a considerable number of double stars and found that the distance between them was usually changing, but not in the way one would expect when observing parallax. Instead, it seemed that the dimmer star was moving in such a way as to seem to be going about the brighter star in an orbit—much in the way a planet goes about a sun.

By 1802 Herschel was convinced that there were many true double stars, and not just stars that seemed close together by virtue of being in the same direction from Earth. These true double stars are usually called "binary stars" from a Latin word meaning "in pairs."

Such binaries are not at all rare. Thousands are now known. Out of every hundred reasonably bright stars taken at random, five or six are likely to prove to be binaries when observed through the telescope. In some cases, stars may seem single even when seen through the telescope, but can be shown to be double in other ways.

Among the first-magnitude stars, Sirius, Capella, Procyon, Alpha Crucis, Castor, Spica, and Antares are binaries. What is most important to us in this book is that Alpha Centauri is not just a double star, either. It, too, is a binary.

Although Herschel's discovery of binary stars was a matter of first-rate astronomical importance, it did not solve the problem of the distance of the stars. It did, however, offer one more way of judging which stars might be nearer than others.

Suppose, for instance, that all binary stars consisted of pairs that were the same distance apart in kilometers. In that case, the farther a binary star is from us, the less separate the pair appears. (This is the same trick of perspective that makes railroad tracks appear to come closer together as you follow them off in the distance.)

This is not a certain measure of distance, of course, because there is no guarantee that binaries always consist of pairs of stars a fixed distance apart. Some binaries may seem to be separated by quite a bit of space because the pair is unusually far apart in actual fact; or they might be closely spaced because the stars are actually closer together than average.

Still, the degree of separation may tell us something. Table 12 shows the distance between the paired stars in certain binaries. (The figures given in the table can be a little misleading. As the paired stars move about each other, they can sometimes be a little closer together than at other times. The exact figure depends on the time when the measurement is made; however, the figures in Table 12 give the general idea.)

There's still another way of judging the closeness of some binary stars as compared with others. It takes time for one star to circle another. If binary stars were all the same size, we could say that the farther apart the paired stars were, the longer it would take them to circle each other. For one thing, they would have to make a larger circle, and for another, they would travel more slowly because the gravitational pull between the stars weakens with distance, and it is the strength of the

TABLE 12

Separation of Binaries

BINARY	SEPARATION OF STARS (SECONDS OF ARC)
Delta Cephei	41.0
Beta Cygni	34.5
Eta Persei	28.0
Theta Serpentis	22.2
Alpha Canum Venaticorum	19.8
Mizar	14.3
Gamma Delphini	10.4
Alpha Centauri	**9.9**
Gamma Andromedae	9.8
Eta Cassiopeiae	9.6
Rigel	9.5
Gamma Arietis	8.0
Sirius	7.6
70 Ophiuchi	6.0
Gamma Virginis	5.5
Alpha Crucis	4.7
Alpha Herculis	4.7
Gamma Leonis	3.9
Delta Serpentis	3.7
Antares	2.9
Epsilon Boötis	2.8
Epsilon Aurigae	2.8
Zeta Aquarii	2.3
Alpha Piscium	2.2
Castor	2.1

gravitational pull that dictates the speed with which an object travels in its orbit.

Suppose a binary pair that looks far apart takes a long time to complete the orbital circle. In that case, they are really far apart.

If a binary pair that looks far apart takes a *short* time to complete the orbital circle, then they are not really far apart, but merely look far apart because they are close. In Table 13, the orbital period (the time it takes for the stars to complete their orbit about each other) is given for some of the stars listed in Table 12.

Eta Cassiopeiae has an apparent separation of its pair very much like that of Alpha Centauri, as you can see in Table 12. However, the Eta Cassiopeiae pair has an orbital period five times that of the Alpha Centauri pair, as you can see in Table 13. From this we can argue that the two stars of Eta Cassiopeiae are, in reality, much farther apart than those of Alpha Centauri. We could then go on to argue that the separation of the two stars of Alpha Centauri seems to be as large as that of Eta Cassiopeiae only because Alpha Centauri is much the closer to the two.

Then, too, Gamma Virginis and 70 Ophiuchi have separations smaller than those of Alpha Centauri and Sirius and yet have longer periods. Gamma Virginis and 70 Ophiuchi might

TABLE 13

Orbital Period of Some Binaries

BINARY	ORBITAL PERIOD (YEARS)
Eta Cassiopeiae	400.9
Gamma Virginis	171.4
70 Ophiuchi	87.85
Alpha Centauri	**80.09**
Sirius	49.94

therefore be farther away from us than are Alpha Centauri and Sirius.

Even this matter of orbital period is not entirely convincing. Two stars may be far apart and yet have a short period because they are large, massive stars. Massive stars possess very strong gravitational fields that can drive objects through their orbits at unusually high velocities.

Still, although each piece of evidence offers us something uncertain, the more such pieces crop up, the less the uncertainty. Alpha Centauri and Sirius are both bright stars, they both have large proper motions, both have fairly wide separations between the two paired stars, and yet both have fairly short orbital periods.

Putting all this together, we can be reasonably sure that Alpha Centauri and Sirius must be among the stars closest to us—and yet nothing short of actually obtaining the parallax will prove this. Before going on to that matter, however, let's take one more look at binaries.

In some cases, the fact that a star is a binary does not much affect our notion of the brightness of the brighter star of the two. If one of the pair is much dimmer than the other, then the bright star contributes just about all the brightness, and its magnitude alone is just about equal to the magnitude of both together.

Consider Sirius, for instance. The dimmer of the pair, Sirius B, has a magnitude of 8.4 and is too dim to see with the unaided eye. Its existence scarcely alters the brightness of the star we see. It is the brighter companion, Sirius A, which is all that counts in this respect. Without any contribution from its dim companion, it alone is the brightest star in the sky. Procyon is another star in which the brighter of the pair, Procyon A, contributes virtually all the light of the two, its companion, Procyon B, having a magnitude of 10.8.

It is also possible, however, for the two stars of a binary to be fairly close to each other in brightness. In that case, the star as we see it is considerably brighter than each one of the pair would be if we could see it separately.

Alpha Crucis, for instance, has a magnitude of 0.90, making it a distinct first-magnitude star. Of its two components, however, the brighter, Alpha Crucis A, with a magnitude of 1.4 is just a borderline first-magnitude star, while Alpha Crucis B, with a magnitude of 1.9, is a second-magnitude star.

Alpha Centauri falls into the second class. Its components are comparable in brightness. Though Alpha Centauri, taking both its stars together, has a magnitude of −0.27, the brighter of the pair, Alpha Centauri A, has a magnitude of 0.4, while Alpha Centauri B has a magnitude of 1.6.

4
DISTANCE
AND
LUMINOSITY

The Nearest Star

Although Herschel had failed in his attempt to determine stellar parallax by way of double stars, efforts in that direction by way of other techniques continued. Telescopes and other instruments were continually being improved, so that smaller and ever smaller shifts in the position of stars could be detected with precision. In the 1830s three different astronomers tackled the problem in a strenuous effort at solution, and each chose a different star.

The German-Russian astronomer Friedrich Georg Wilhelm von Struve (fun-SHTROO-vuh) decided to go for brightness as a criterion for closeness. His observatory was at 58.2° N on the shores of the Baltic Sea, and only bright stars with a large positive declination were high in the sky there. He therefore picked the most northerly of the five brightest stars, Vega, and concentrated on trying to detect its tiny shift in position in the sky (compared to nearby faint stars) as Earth traveled along its path about the sun.

The German astronomer Friedrich Wilhelm Bessel (BESsul) used rapid proper motion as a criterion for closeness. He therefore concentrated on 61 Cygni, the fastest-moving star known at the time, and compared its position from day to day and month to month relative to those of two nearby dimmer stars that had no detectable proper motion. He assumed that those two neighboring stars were very far away and would show no parallax at all.

The Scottish astronomer Thomas Henderson decided to go for a combination of promising properties. He was manning an observatory at the Cape of Good Hope, near the southernmost tip of Africa, and from there he had an excellent view of the far southern star Alpha Centauri. Keeping in mind that star's brightness, its high proper motion, and the short period of the two separate stars that made it up, he decided to concentrate on that.

As it happened, all three astronomers succeeded in detecting stellar parallax at last. Of the three, Henderson completed the work first, but he didn't stop to analyze his observations and calculate the parallax (a long and tedious job in the days before computers) until after he had completed his job at the Cape and had returned to Scotland. He had no way of knowing, you see, that two other astronomers were hot on his heels.

Henderson's delay meant that Bessel had time to analyze his observations and to announce the results in 1838. He was the first of the three to make the announcement and the credit, in science, goes to the one who first announces. Therefore Bessel is considered to be the first person to have determined the distance of a star.

The stellar parallax is measured as the maximum distance of a star from its average position over the year, and it is given in seconds of arc. For instance, Bessel found that 61 Cygni marked out a tiny ellipse in the sky as the Earth shifted its position in going about the sun, and that the farthest distance of this ellipse from its center was 0.3″. This is the stellar parallax of 61 Cygni. (Actually, the best measurement for the parallax, as we now have it, is 0.293″.)

Knowing the parallax of 61 Cygni and the width of Earth's

orbit, it is possible to calculate the distance of 61 Cygni, which turns out to be 11.1 light-years. This is equal to about 106 trillion kilometers (65 trillion miles) or just about 700,000 A.U.

Another unit sometimes used to measure the distance of a star is the "parsec." This is the distance at which a star would have a parallax of exactly 1 second of arc, and the word is an abbreviation of "parallax-second." To have a parallax of 1″, a star would have to be at a distance of 3.258 light-years, which is equal to about 31 trillion kilometers (19 trillion miles), or 206,000 A.U.

We can say that 61 Cygni, being 11.1 light-years from us, is 3.42 parsecs away.

Henderson found the parallax of Alpha Centauri to be greater than that of 61 Cygni. The best value we have today is 0.756″, which means that Alpha Centauri is 4.40 light-years from us, or 1.35 parsecs.

Of the three stars whose parallax was first determined, Vega, which came in third, was the most distant. It is now thought to be 27 light-years away, or 8.3 parsecs.

Since 1838, scores of stars have had their distance measured by the method of parallax but (with a partial exception we'll come to soon) no star has proved to be closer to our sun and its planets than Alpha Centauri. Alpha Centauri is our nearest star neighbor in space. This means that there is no star that has a parallax of over 1″ (as far as we know), and no star that is less than a parsec distant from us.

When we say that Alpha Centauri is the nearest star, we must not forget that we are using the name to refer to a binary system. It is actually two individual stars, Alpha Centauri A and Alpha Centauri B. Each takes turns being a trifle the closer to us as they rotate about each other. The difference in closeness is so small, however, and the changeabout, as they revolve, so frequent that the matter is ignored and neither Alpha Centauri A nor Alpha Centauri B is ever singled out as the nearest star. The two would share the honors except for one thing—

Alpha Centauri turns out to have a third component. It is a "ternary" star, from a Latin word for "three." In 1913 Robert Innes, a British astronomer in South Africa, discovered a very dim star of the eleventh magnitude that also had a high parallax, very much like that of Alpha Centauri. Since it was only about 2° away from Alpha Centauri, there was a chance that it might be part of the multiple-star system. A study of its motion over the years makes it look as if this is indeed so.

At the distance of Alpha Centauri, a 2° difference in position in the sky represents a distance of 0.15 light-years. Innes's dim star, then, which we can call Alpha Centauri C, must be about 1.6 trillion kilometers (1 trillion miles) from the two chief stars of the system. This is about 270 times the distance of Pluto from our sun, or 10,000 times the distance of Earth from our sun. It would take Alpha Centauri C well over a million years to complete one turn of its orbit about the main stars.

The orbit of Alpha Centauri C is so arranged in space that in moving around the two main stars, Alpha Centauri C is sometimes quite a bit closer to us than they are and sometimes quite a bit farther. In its case, the difference is noticeable and the changeovers from closer to farther and back again come only at long intervals.

At the moment, as it happens, Alpha Centauri C is in a part of its orbit that brings it considerably closer to us than the main stars are. It has been in that part of the orbit through all the history of civilization and will continue to be there for many tens of thousands of years. Its parallax is 0.762″ as compared to 0.756″ for the main stars, and its distance from us is 4.27 light-years (1.31 parsecs) as compared to 4.40 light-years (1.35) parsecs for the main stars.

Because of this, Alpha Centauri C is sometimes called "Proxima Centauri" (PROK-sih-muh) from the Latin word for "nearest."

Our Neighbors

In Table 14 are listed all the stars known to be within 13 light years (4 parsecs) of our solar system. We see from Table 14 that the various indications mentioned toward the end of the previous chapter were correct. Alpha Centauri and Sirius are indeed our closest neighbors among the bright stars—and it is (in part, at least) because they are so close that they seem so bright.

Yet closeness isn't enough. Of the thirty close stars (counting the two stars of binary systems separately) only four—Alpha Centauri A, Alpha Centauri B, Sirius A, and Procyon A—are among the bright stars. Five more—Epsilon Eridani, 61 Cygni A, Cygni B, Epsilon Indi, and Tau Ceti—are not bright but are still visible to the unaided eye. The remaining 21 of the close stars, 70 percent of the total, are so dim, despite their closeness, that they cannot be seen without a telescope.

It seems very unlikely that our solar system just happens to be surrounded by dim stars in an exceptional manner. It seems much more likely that dim stars are of very common occurrence everywhere; that most stars are too dim to make out even by telescope unless relatively close to the observer; and that bright stars are exceptional.

The only dim stars we can see, even by telescope, are quite close. The farther off we penetrate with our instruments, the more we see only bright objects—so that by trusting to our senses alone, we get a false idea of the brightness of the starry universe.

In Table 15 the distances of the various first-magnitude stars are given. The farthest of them is at least 540 light-years (165 parsecs) away. Within that distance (judging from the number of stars in our neighborhood) there must be about 20 million

TABLE 14

Our Nearest Neighbors

	DISTANCE	
STAR	LIGHT-YEARS	PARSECS
Alpha Centauri C	**4.27**	**1.31**
Alpha Centauri A & B	**4.40**	**1.35**
Barnard's Star	5.86	1.81
Wolf 359	7.66	2.35
Lalande 21185	8.21	2.52
Sirius A & B	8.63	2.65
Luyten 726-8 A & B	8.86	2.72
Ross 154	9.45	2.90
Epsilon Eridani	10.7	3.28
Luyten 789.6	10.8	3.31
Ross 128	10.8	3.31
61 Cygni A & B	11.2	3.44
Epsilon Indi	11.2	3.44
Procyon A & B	11.4	3.50
Sigma 2398 A & B	11.5	3.53
Groombridge 34 A & B	11.6	3.56
Lacaille 9352	11.7	3.59
Tau Ceti	11.9	3.65
+5° 1668	12.4	3.81
Lacaille 8760	12.8	3.93
Kapteyn's Star	13.0	4.02
Ross 614	13.1	4.02
Krüger 60	13.1	4.02

stars at least, and all but a few thousand of the brightest are invisible to the unaided eyes. Most, in fact, are invisible even to our telescopes.

The greater the distance of a star, the smaller the parallax, and the harder it is to measure it accurately. Therefore, though we can be quite certain of the distance of the nearer stars, the distance of the farther stars becomes rather fuzzy. The distance figures for the half-dozen farthest stars in Table 15 are rather rough, and yet even those stars are very close to us by comparison to most of the stars in the universe.

Most of the stars and star collections in the universe are thousands, or millions, or even billions of light-years away, and their distances must be determined by methods other than parallax. Those distant stars, however, are not the subjects under discussion in this book. Here we are concerned only with the nearer stars.

Allowing for Distance

One thing that stands out in Table 15 is the remarkable brightness of some of the more distant stars. Consider Rigel. It is about 50 times as far from us as Procyon is, and yet Rigel shines more brightly in the sky than Procyon does. (For that matter, Rigel is about 120 times as far away as Alpha Centauri is, yet the two stars are not very different in apparent brightness.)

The intensity of light decreases as does the square of the distance. That means that if two stars are emitting light in equal amounts, but if one is fifty times farther away from us than the other (as Rigel is 50 times farther away than Procyon), then the more distant star appears less bright by the square of 50; that is, by 50 × 50, or 2,500 times. Yet Rigel is not dimmer at all; it is brighter than Procyon. Rigel must therefore give out more than 2,500 times as much light as Procyon, so that even its 50-fold distance does not dim it to the Procyon level.

We can work it the other way. Alpha Centauri C is much dimmer than Alpha Centauri A or B, although Alpha Centauri C is a bit closer to us than the other two components of the system are. We can only assume that Alpha Centauri C emits far less light than Alpha Centauri A or Alpha Centauri B.

TABLE 15

Distances of the Bright Stars

STAR	DISTANCE	
	LIGHT-YEARS	PARSECS
Alpha Centauri	**4.40**	**1.35**
Sirius	8.63	2.65
Procyon	11.43	3.51
Altair	15.7	4.82
Fomalhaut	23	7.1
Vega	27	8.3
Pollux	33	10.1
Arcturus	40	12.3
Capella	42	12.9
Castor	45	13.8
Aldebaran	55	16.9
Achernar	70	21.5
Regulus	77	23.6
Canopus	100	31
Beta Centauri	190	58
Spica	190	58
Alpha Crucis	220	68
Antares	220	68
Betelgeuse	325	100
Deneb	400	123
Rigel	540	165

In short, once the distances of various stars was determined, it was quickly discovered that the difference in the brightness of the stars in the sky was not entirely due to differences in distance. There was also a difference in the amount of light they emitted.

The difference in the amount of light emitted by various stars can be made clearer if we pretend that all the stars are at some particular distance from us and calculate what their magnitudes would be then.

For instance, Alpha Centauri has a magnitude of −0.27 and a distance of 1.35 parsecs. Suppose we imagined it at a distance of 10 parsecs, which is 7.4 times its real distance. Since we are imagining it farther away, it would seem dimmer at its new distance; its brightness decreasing 7.4 × 7.4, or 55 times. From that decrease in brightness, we could calculate what its magnitude would be at 10 parsecs.

On the other hand, imagine that Rigel, which has a magnitude of 0.14 at a distance of 165 parsecs, is also at a distance of 10 parsecs. Since it is being imagined closer than it really is, it would appear brighter. Its increase in brightness would be 16.5 × 16.5, or 272 times, and from that its magnitude at 10 parsecs can be calculated.

The magnitude that any star would have if it were at a distance of 10 parsecs from us is called its "absolute magnitude." What we have been calling simply the "magnitude" so far in the book—the brightness of a star at whatever distance it happens to be in fact—is sometimes called the "apparent magnitude."

In Table 16 the absolute magnitudes of the brightest stars are given.

A star with a low apparent magnitude is said to be "bright"; a star with a low absolute magnitude is said to be "luminous." Thus, of all the stars we can see with the unaided eye, Sirius A is the brightest, but Rigel is the most luminous.

There is no star brighter than Sirius A, for brightness is something apparent to the eyes and we can *see* that there is no star brighter than Sirius A. On the other hand, a star can be very luminous and yet be so far away that it can't even be seen at all with the unaided eye. There is no reason to think, then, that among all the billions of stars not visible to the unaided eye, there may not be many stars more luminous than

TABLE 16

Absolute Magnitude of the Bright Stars

STAR	ABSOLUTE MAGNITUDE
Rigel	—6.2
Deneb	—4.8
Canopus	—4.6
Betelgeuse	—4.3
Beta Centauri	—3.1
Alpha Crucis A	—2.7
Achernar	—2.6
Antares A	—2.4
Spica	—2.2
Alpha Crucis B	—2.2
Regulus A	—0.7
Capella A	—0.5
Aldebaran A	—0.5
Arcturus	0.0
Vega	0.5
Pollux	1.0
Sirius A	1.3
Antares B	1.6
Fomalhaut	2.1
Altair	2.4
Procyon A	2.8
Alpha Centauri A	**4.7**

Rigel. The trouble is that unless we know the actual distance of a star we can't calculate its luminosity, and we know the distance of only a very few stars.

We do know, though, of one star that is definitely more luminous than Rigel, even though it is invisible to the unaided eye.

In the constellation Dorado, in the southern half of the sky (and therefore invisible to people in the United States or in Europe), there is the Large Magellanic Cloud. This is a collection of millions of stars that are all so far away that to the unaided eye all those stars appear only as a small patch of dim foggy light. The distance of the Large Magellanic Cloud has been determined by methods other than parallax, and it turns out to be 150,000 light-years (45,000 parsecs) away from us, or 34,000 times as distant as Alpha Centauri.

Through the telescope, some of the stars of the Large Magellanic Cloud can be made out, and the brightest of these is one named "S Doradus." At its vast distance, S Doradus reduces to a tiny speck of light indeed, but that it can shine even as brightly as it does at the vast distance of 150,000 light-years is remarkable. If S Doradus were viewed from a distance of only 10 parsecs, it would turn out to have an absolute magnitude of about −9.5. (There are also occasions when a star explodes and when, for a short time, it can reach a peak of brightness equivalent to an absolute magnitude of −14.)

Restricting ourselves to non-exploding stars visible to the unaided eyes, however, it turns out that there are no fewer than sixteen familiar stars that are more luminous than Sirius A. In fact, Alpha Crucis A and Alpha Crucis B, the two components of the binary Alpha Crucis, are *each* more luminous than Sirius. (Rigel, however, is far more luminous than both components of Alpha Crucis put together.)

Alpha Centauri's brightness in the sky, on the other hand, is largely a tribute to its unusual closeness. Of all the first-magnitude stars, Alpha Centauri is the least luminous. At a distance of ten parsecs, Alpha Centauri A would be a very ordinary dim star, and Alpha Centauri B, which is even dimmer, would be barely visible to the unaided eye on a dark, clear, moonless night. (If Rigel were at the distance of Alpha Centauri, on the other hand, it would be an enormously brilliant spot of light, with a brightness almost equal to that of the full moon. It would probably damage the eye to look at Rigel if it were as close as Alpha Centauri.)

Before we feel too disappointed in Alpha Centauri, however, let's consider our own sun. It is far brighter than all the stars visible to the unaided eye put together, but what about its luminosity? After all, the sun is so close to us compared to the stars that perhaps its brightness is entirely due to its closeness and it isn't very luminous at all.

The sun is only 0.0000158 light-years (0.0000048 parsecs) from the Earth. If it were imagined at a distance of 10 parsecs, it would have an absolute magnitude of 4.69. In other words, though Alpha Centauri A doesn't cut much of a figure compared to the other first-magnitude stars, it is nevertheless as luminous as our sun—or, if you care to look at it that way, our sun is as unremarkable a star as is Alpha Centauri A.

However, before we sneer too readily at either Alpha Centauri A or the sun, let us consider that there are stars far less luminous than either, as is evidenced by the examples given in Table 17. Furthermore, remember that dim stars are far more numerous than bright ones, and that distant stars are far more numerous than close ones. The common occurrence of both dimness and great distance means that most stars are invisible to us and that prominent bright stars are very unusual. Don't give too much weight, therefore, to the existence of those very few stars with the great luminosity of a Rigel or an S Doradus. About 90 percent of the stars that exist are less luminous than either the sun or Alpha Centauri A.

Luminosity Extremes

It is, of course, rather difficult to get an idea of luminosity from magnitudes alone, since each magnitude represents a multiple of the one before.

Thus, suppose a particular star is one magnitude brighter than another. That particular star is 2.512 times as bright. A

TABLE 17

Absolute Magnitude of Some Dim Stars

STAR	ABSOLUTE MAGNITUDE
Alpha Centauri A	**4.7**
Sun	4.7
Regulus B	5.6
70 Ophiuchi A	5.8
Tau Ceti	5.9
Alpha Centauri B	**6.1**
Epsilon Eridani	6.2
Epsilon Indi	7.0
70 Ophiuchi B	7.5
61 Cygni A	7.9
61 Cygni B	8.6
Capella B	9.3
Sirius B	10.0
Kapteyn's Star	10.8
Regulus C	11.0
Aldebaran B	11.4
Procyon B	13.1
Barnard's Star	13.3
Van Maanen's Star	14.3
Alpha Centauri C	**15.4**
Wolf 359	16.6
Van Biesbroeck's Star	19.2

star that is two magnitudes brighter than another is 2.512 × 2.512 or 6.31 times as bright. A star that is three magnitudes brighter than another is 2.512× 2.512 × 2.512 or 15.85 times as bright.

Suppose, therefore, that we consider the luminosity directly. Never mind how many absolute magnitudes brighter or dimmer than the sun a particular star might be; let us calculate instead how much more (or less) light it delivers—how much more (or less) luminous it is.

For instance, Procyon A has an absolute magnitude just 1.9 brighter than Alpha Centauri A. That means Procyon A is 5.8 times as luminous as Alpha Centauri A. It would take 5.8 stars like Alpha Centauri A to produce as much light as Procyon A does.

On the other hand, the absolute magnitude of Alpha Centauri A is 2.3 brighter than that of Epsilon Indi. This means that Alpha Centauri A is 8.1 times as luminous as Epsilon Indi, or that Epsilon Indi is 0.12 as luminous as Alpha Centauri A.

Table 18 lists the luminosities of some stars that are more luminous than Alpha Centauri A or the sun; Table 19 gives the luminosities of some that are less luminous than Alpha Centauri A or the sun.

We can see from Table 18 that Sirius A is 23 times as bright as Alpha Centauri A or the sun. Actually, this is not surprising. Halley had calculated it should be two light-years from us if it were as bright as our sun. The fact that it is over eight light-years away means at once that it must be considerably brighter than the sun to appear as bright as it does.

If Alpha Centauri A were substituted for our sun, the person in the street probably couldn't tell the difference. If Sirius A were substituted for our sun, however, the vast flood of additional light and heat would boil our oceans away and make Earth uninhabitable. In order for Sirius A to appear to us only as bright as the sun does now, Earth would have to circle it at a distance of 720,000,000 kilometers (450,000,000 miles), as compared to its distance from the sun of 150,000,000 kilometers (93,000,000 miles). Roughly speaking, Sirius A, if substituted for the sun, would appear from the distance of Jupiter as the sun appears at the distance of Earth.

Imagine Rigel in place of the sun. Earth would have to

TABLE 18

Luminosities of Some Bright Stars

STAR	LUMINOSITY (SUN = 1)
S Doradus	480,000
Rigel	23,000
Deneb	6,300
Canopus	5,200
Betelgeuse	4,400
Beta Centauri	1,300
Alpha Crucis A	910
Achernar	830
Antares A	690
Spica	570
Alpha Crucis B	570
Regulus A	140
Capella A	120
Aldebaran A	120
Arcturus	76
Vega	48
Pollux	30
Sirius A	23
Antares B	17
Fomalhaut	11
Altair	8.3
Procyon A	5.8
Alpha Centauri A	**1.0**
Sun	1.0

circle it at a distance of 23,000,000,000 kilometers (14,000,000,-000 miles) in order to bring its light down to the level of the sun as we see it from Earth. This would be about four times

TABLE 19

Luminosities of Some Dim Stars

STAR	LUMINOSITY (SUN = 1)
Alpha Centauri A	**1.0**
Sun	1.0
Regulus B	0.44
70 Ophiuchi A	0.36
Tau Ceti	0.33
Alpha Centauri B	**0.28**
Epsilon Eridani	0.25
Epsilon Indi	0.12
70 Ophiuchi B	0.076
61 Cygni A	0.053
61 Cygni B	0.028
Capella B	0.014
Sirius B	0.0076
Kapteyn's Star	0.0036
Regulus C	0.0030
Aldebaran B	0.0021
Procyon B	0.00044
Barnard's Star	0.00036
Van Maanen's Star	0.00014
Alpha Centauri C	**0.000053**
Wolf 359	0.000017
Van Biesbroeck's Star	0.0000015

the distance of Pluto. In other words, place Rigel where our sun is and even Pluto would become unendurably hot from the human standpoint.

S Doradus in place of the sun would force a retreat to a

distance of 105,000,000,000 kilometers (65,000,000,000 miles), or about 17 times the distance of Pluto.

Think of this, and you may decide that Alpha Centauri A is not disappointingly dim at all. Rather, it is a pleasant home-like star that is the comfortable twin of our sun.

And what of the less luminous stars? Suppose that Van Biesbroeck's star (called by that name because it was first discovered by the Belgian-American astronomer George Van Biesbroeck) were substituted for the sun. It is the dimmest known star and is only about 1/670,000 as bright as the sun. It would not deliver enough light and heat to keep the Earth's oceans from freezing solid. It would shine in our sky like a small dim-red marble only three quarters as bright as the full moon seems to us now. (And with that tiny sun in our sky, the moon would receive so little light that it would be barely visible.)

In order for Earth to get as much light from Van Biesbroeck's star as it now gets from the sun, Earth would have to circle Van Biesbroeck's star at a distance of about 183,000 kilometers (113,500 miles). It would have to be closer to that tiny sun than the moon is, now, to the Earth.

Both extremes are unbearable and we are fortunate that the sun is as it is, an average star.

It might seem to you that this is a narrow way of looking at it. You might think that we are comfortable with the sun because we are used to it the way it is, and that if we happened to have a considerably larger sun or a considerably smaller one, we would be used to that, and think the large sun or the small sun was just right.

Actually, as we shall see later in the book, the average star is right for us, and not just because we're used to it.

5
DISTANCE
AND
SIZE

Binary Systems

Once astronomers determined the distance of stars, it became possible to tell some things about size. They could, for instance, calculate the dimensions of binary systems.

If a binary system is observed over the years, the shift in position of the two stars relative to each other can be plotted, and a little diagram can be drawn of the way in which they move. The separation of the two stars in seconds of arc can be measured and, if the distance is known, this can be converted into actual kilometers.

The magnificent binary system of Alpha Crucis, for instance, consists of two stars about 80 billion kilometers (50 billion miles) apart. One of them is 910 times as bright as the sun and the other 570 times as bright.

Table 20 lists the average distance between the two stars of a number of other binary systems. To give you an idea of the size of the separations in terms of our own, more familiar, solar system, the various planets are given with their distances from our sun, and are placed in the appropriate positions in the table.

The stars listed in Table 20 are just a sampling, and the figures for many of the systems given are of only limited accuracy.

TABLE 20

Size of Binary Systems

STAR	DISTANCE OF SEPARATION	
	KILOMETERS	MILES
Delta Cygni	16,000,000,000	10,000,000,000
Castor	11,400,000,000	7,100,000,000
Eta Cassiopeiae	9,700,000,000	6,000,000,000
Phi Ursae Majoris	6,900,000,000	4,300,000,000
Gamma Virginis	6,800,000,000	4,200,000,000
(Pluto-Sun)	(5,900,000,000)	(3,670,000,000)
(Neptune-Sun)	(4,500,000,000)	(2,800,000,000)
Alpha Ursae Majoris	4,300,000,000	2,700,000,000
70 Ophiuchi	3,500,000,000	2,200,000,000
Zeta Sagittarii	3,500,000,000	2,200,000,000
Alpha Centauri	**3,500,000,000**	**2,200,000,000**
Eta Ophiuchi	3,200,000,000	2,000,000,000
Zeta Cancri	3,150,000,000	1,960,000,000
Sirius	3,000,000,000	1,900,000,000
Xi Scorpii	3,000,000,000	1,900,000,000
(Uranus-Sun)	(2,870,000,000)	(1,780,000,000)
Procyon	2,250,000,000	1,400,000,000
Zeta Herculis	2,040,000,000	1,270,000,000
Eta Coronae Borealis	1,870,000,000	1,160,000,000
42 Comae	1,840,000,000	1,140,000,000
Epsilon Hydrae	1,650,000,000	1,030,000,000
(Saturn-Sun)	(1,400,000,000)	(890,000,000)
(Jupiter-Sun)	(777,000,000)	(483,000,000)
Delta Equulei	620,000,000	385,000,000
Beta Capricorni	375,000,000	234,000,000
(Mars-Sun)	(228,000,000)	(142,000,000)
(Earth-Sun)	(150,000,000)	(93,000,000)
(Venus-Sun)	(108,000,000)	(67,000,000)

| | DISTANCE OF SEPARATION | |
STAR	KILOMETERS	MILES
Capella	84,000,000	52,000,000
(Mercury-Sun)	(58,000,000)	(36,000,000)

The separation of the two stars of Delta Cygni is nearly three times as great as the distance of Pluto from the sun, but there are separations greater than that, too. After all, Alpha Centauri C is separated from Alpha Centauri A and B by just about 1,600 billion kilometers (1 trillion miles). This distance is over 250 times that of Pluto from the sun and about 100 times that separating the two stars of Delta Cygni.

At the other extreme, the two stars making up the Mizar binary system are closer to each other than Mercury is to the sun, and yet there are binaries in which the two stars are considerably closer even than that. The really close pairs cannot be made out separately by eye even with the help of the telescope. Fortunately, as we shall see, there are other instruments available.

In the case of the Alpha Centauri system, the average separation of the two stars Alpha Centauri A and Alpha Centauri B is greater than that of Uranus and the sun, and less than that of Neptune and the sun. If the Alpha Centauri system were superimposed on the solar system, however, with Alpha Centauri A in place of our sun, Alpha Centauri B would not take up a circular orbit between those of Uranus and Neptune. Things would be a little more complicated than that.

If the orbit of an object moving around a star were an exact circle, the star would remain at the precise center of the orbit and that would represent a very simple situation. Actually, the orbit is always an ellipse, a kind of flattened circle. An ellipse has a major axis (its longest diameter) and a minor axis (its

FIGURE 1

Circles and Ellipses

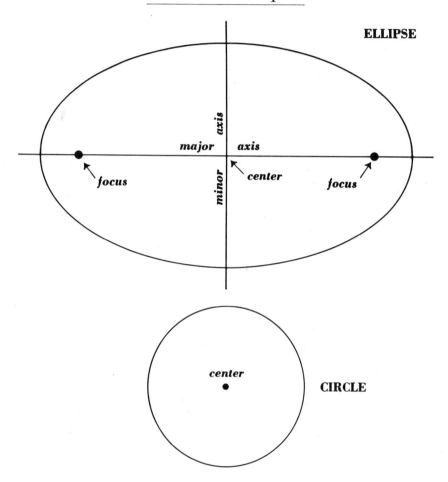

shortest diameter). The center of the ellipse is at the point where the two axes cross (see Figure 1).

There are two focus points, or foci, in the ellipse. They are located on the major axis, one on each side of the center and at equal distances from it. The more flattened the ellipse, the farther the foci are from the center and the closer they are to the ends.

These foci are located in such a way that if a straight line is drawn from one focus to any point on the ellipse, and from that point another straight line is drawn to the other focus, the sum of the lengths of the two straight lines is always equal, and always equal in size to the major axis too.

As it happens, when an object moves about a star in an elliptical orbit, the star is always at one of the foci and is, therefore, nearer to one end of the orbit than to the other. If the ellipse is very flattened, the star is far to one end, and the orbiting object is very close to the star at that end of the orbit and very far from it at the other end.

The point of close approach is called the "periastron" (PEHR-ee-AS-tron) from Greek words meaning "near the star." The point of farthest position is the "apastron" (ap-AS-tron), from Greek words meaning "away from the star" (see Figure 2).

FIGURE 2

Periastron and Apastron

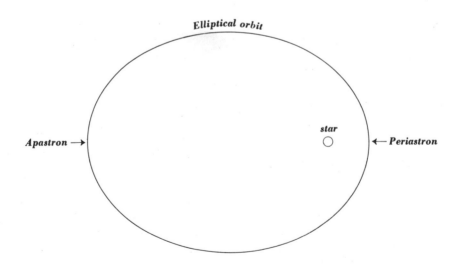

Elliptical orbit

star

Apastron →   ← *Periastron*

In binary systems both stars, under the pull of gravity, move in an orbit about a position between them called the "center of gravity." As they move, both stars always remain on opposite sides of the center of gravity, and the larger star is always closer to it. This means that although both stars have orbits that are ellipses of the same shape, the larger star always moves through the smaller orbit.

When one object in a binary system is very much larger than the other, it makes such a small ellipse about the center of gravity that it is practically stationary. That is the case of the sun and Earth, for instance, where the sun scarcely moves at all while the tiny Earth moves in a large ellipse.

It is always possible, however, to suppose that the larger of two objects in a binary system is standing still and to calculate the orbit of the smaller about it. This distorts the situation relative to observers in other planetary systems—relative to us, for instance. However, if we could imagine ourselves observing the binary system from the larger of the two stars, what we would observe would be the smaller star moving about a motionless larger one.

When astronomers observe the binary systems, they are not at all likely to be viewing it from exactly up above, so to speak, so as to see the elliptical orbits marked out exactly as they are. They usually view the orbits from a tilted position so that the ellipses they see are not the ellipses marked out by the orbiting stars. What they see are ellipses that are more flattened, sometimes very much more flattened. In these distorted ellipses, however, the larger star, which is supposed to be stationary, is not at the focus of the smaller star's orbit. If astronomers tilt the orbit, in imagination, until the star moves into the focus, they get the true ellipse.

Eccentricity

The degree of flattening of an ellipse is measured as its "eccentricity" (from Greek words meaning "out of center"), since the greater the eccentricity, the farther the foci are from the center. The eccentricity of a circle, which is not flattened at all, is 0. For an ellipse, the eccentricity is always between 0 and 1. If an ellipse has a low eccentricity of, say, less than 0.1, it is so slightly flattened that to the eye it looks very much like a circle. As an ellipse is more and more flattened, it approaches closer and closer to a value of 1. By the time an eccentricity of 0.9 is reached, the orbit looks quite cigar-shaped.

An example of a high degree of eccentricity in a binary system is that of Gamma Virginis, where the eccentricity is 0.88. This means that the distance from the center of the ellipse to the focus is 0.88 times the distance from the center of the ellipse to the end. With the larger star at one focus, the end of the orbit of the other star in the direction of that focus (the periastron) is only 0.12 times the distance from the center and only 0.06 times the entire width of the ellipse from end to end. The other end of the ellipse (the apastron) is distant from the larger star by an amount equal to 0.94 times the entire width of the ellipse.

In the case of Gamma Virginis, then, although the average distance separating the two stars of the binary is 6,800,000,000 kilometers (4,200,000,000 miles), at periastron the distance of separation is only 810,000,000 kilometers (500,000,000 miles) while at apastron it is 12,800,000,000 kilometers (7,900,000,000 miles).

In other words, the two stars of Gamma Virginis, as they circle each other, swoop together to a separating distance equal to that of Jupiter and the sun, and then move apart to a distance more than twice that of Pluto and the sun. (The system was at apastron in 1920 and the two stars have been moving closer ever since. They will be at periastron in 2006.)

In general, stars separated by quite a large average distance are likely to have large eccentricities. A binary like Capella with an average separation of only 84,000,000 kilometers (52,-000,000 miles) has quite a low eccentricity, one of only 0.0086.

This means that the distance between the two stars of the Capella system varies from 83,300,000 kilometers (51,600,000 miles) at periastron to 84,700,000 kilometers (52,400,000 miles) at apastron.

This is so small a change that from the standpoint of one of the stars of the Capella system, the other would scarcely seem to change in brightness during the 104-day period of revolution. In the case of Gamma Virginis, on the other hand, an observer near one of the stars would see the other to be 250 times as bright at periastron as at apastron.

The eccentricities of the planetary orbits of the solar system, by the way, are much more like those of the Capella stars than those of the Gamma Virginis stars. The eccentricities of the orbits of Venus and Neptune are just about that of the Capella system, while that of Earth (0.017) is only a little higher. This is a good thing, too, for a highly eccentric orbit would introduce such changes in temperature in the course of the year that a planet with a suitable average distance from its sun might prove uninhabitable even so.

Let us take, now, the group of binaries in Table 20 which have average separations of about 3.0 to 3.5 billion kilometers (1.9 to 2.2 billion miles), a group that includes the Alpha Centauri system. In Table 21, the eccentricity and the distances at periastron and apastron are given for this group.

As you see, the apastrons are not extraordinarily different, varying from 4,100 to 6,080 million kilometers (2,570 to 3,800 million miles), a difference of only about 50 percent. The periastrons differ, however, from 320 to 2,700 million kilometers (200 to 1,700 miles), a difference of 800 percent.

The Alpha Centauri system is rather intermediate with respect to eccentricity. The orbits of the two stars Alpha Centauri A and B are more eccentric than those of the planets of our solar system, but less eccentric than those of some of the comets, asteroids, and satellites of our solar system.

If Alpha Centauri A were in the place of our sun, then Alpha

TABLE 21

Eccentricities of Binary Systems

STAR SYSTEM	ECCEN- TRICITY	PERIASTRON		APASTRON	
		MILLIONS OF KILOMETERS	MILLIONS OF MILES	MILLIONS OF KILOMETERS	MILLIONS OF MILES
70 Ophiuchi	0.50	1750	1100	5250	3300
Zeta Sagittarii	0.2	2700	1700	4300	2700
Alpha Centauri	**0.521**	**1700**	**1000**	**5300**	**3400**
Eta Ophiuchi	0.90	320	200	6080	3800
Zeta Cancri	0.31	2200	1350	4100	2570
Sirius	0.575	1280	800	4720	3000
Xi Scorpii	0.74	780	500	5200	3300

Centauri B at its farthest would be 5,300,000,000 kilometers (3,400,000,000 miles) away, or just about at the average distance of Pluto from our sun. From Earth's position near Alpha Centauri A, Alpha Centauri B would seem a starlike point, but it would be far brighter than any star we see in our own sky. It would shine with a brilliance about 100 times greater than our full moon, though it would still be only 1/4500 as bright as Alpha Centauri A would be in the place of our sun (or our sun itself is right now).

From its farthest point, however, Alpha Centauri B would slowly decrease its distance to Alpha Centauri A (and ourselves) as it moved along its orbit (see Figure 3) until after forty years it would be at periastron and only 1,700,000,000 kilometers (1,000,000,000 miles) from Alpha Centauri A. At that point it would be a little farther from Alpha Centauri A than Saturn is from the sun. And when Earth would be on the side of its orbit toward Alpha Centauri B, the companion star would be only 1,550,000,000 kilometers (900,000,000 miles) from us.

FIGURE 3

The Orbit of Alpha Centauri B
(superimposed on our solar system)

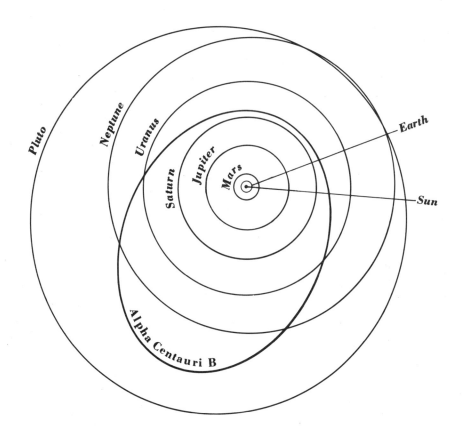

At that distance, Alpha Centauri B would be a little over 14 times as bright as at apastron. It would be 1400 times as bright as the full moon, but still only 1/326 as bright as Alpha Centauri A.

Suppose it were Alpha Centauri B that was in place of our sun, and that we calculated the orbit of Alpha Centauri A on the assumption that Alpha Centauri B was motionless. Alpha

Centauri A would then seem to move in the same orbit that Alpha Centauri B had moved in the other case.*

Alpha Centauri A would go through the same period of brightening as it moved from apastron to periastron, viewed from an Earth that was circling Alpha Centauri B instead of our own sun, and the same period of dimming as it moved back to apastron. However, since Alpha Centauri A is 3¼ times as bright as Alpha Centauri B, Alpha Centauri A would seem that much brighter at every point in its orbit. At its brightest, it would be 5,000 times brighter than our full moon now, and 1/100 as bright as our sun appears to us. Since Alpha Centauri B would appear dimmer than the sun, if we imagined the former in the latter's place, Alpha Centauri A at its closest approach would appear 1/30 as bright as Alpha Centauri B.

If we were circling Alpha Centauri A instead of the sun, the presence of Alpha Centauri B would cause us no trouble. Despite the eccentricity of its orbit that allows Alpha Centauri B to swoop in and pull out in forty-year alternations, it would remain so far away at all times that its gravitational pull would never be strong enough to affect Earth's orbit seriously. What's more, its addition to the light and heat delivered by Alpha Centauri A would never be more than a third of one percent. And think of what a marvelous spectacle it would make in the sky.

If we were circling Alpha Centauri B, the superior brightness of Alpha Centauri A would be more disturbing, but if we imagined Earth pulled in closer to Alpha Centauri B in order to receive as much heat and light from that smaller sun as we receive from our own sun, the interference of Alpha Centauri A would not be too disturbing.

---

* Because Alpha Centauri B is the smaller of the two stars, it seems to move in the larger orbit of the two when viewed from *outside* the system. When viewed from inside the system, however, an observer on each star would see the other moving in the same orbit. Thus, on Earth, if we pretend that the Earth is motionless, the sun moves in an orbit about the Earth that is just like the orbit that the Earth (in reality) moves in as it circles the sun.

And what about Alpha Centauri C—Proxima Centauri? Even though it would be far nearer to us, if Earth were circling either Alpha Centauri A or Alpha Centauri B, than any star is to us in our own solar system, it would not be at all bright. It would be a fairly dim star of magnitude 3.7. What's more, its proper motion, as a result of its possibly 1,300,000-year-long revolution around the center of gravity of the two large stars of the system, would be just about 1 second of arc per year.

Neither its brightness nor its proper motion would attract much attention, and stargazers might look at the sky forever and not suspect this dim star of belonging to their own system. The only giveaway would come when astronomers decided to make a routine check of the parallaxes of the various visible stars in the sky. After a month or so, they would begin to get a hint of an extraordinarily large parallax and in the end they would measure one of 20 seconds of arc, which would be so much higher than that of any other star that they would at once suspect it of being a member of their own system.

Can there be a dim star somewhere out there that belongs to our own solar system? Can it be that we remain unaware of it because astronomers haven't happened to study it closely enough to detect an unusually high parallax? It isn't very likely—but it is conceivable.

Mass

Binary stars make it possible to compute the masses of at least some stars; but first we must explain what we mean by "mass."

One way of defining mass is to consider it the measure of the strength of the gravitational field produced by any object. If one object has twice the mass of another, it produces a gravitational field which, at some particular distance, is twice as intense as that of the other. In reverse, if we can measure the gravitational fields of two bodies and find that the field of the first is twice as intense as that of the second, we know that the mass of the first is twice as great as that of the second.

The gravitational attraction between two objects depends on the product of the two masses. If one of the objects remains unchanged, and if its gravitational attraction to various other objects is measured, the amount of attraction depends on the mass of each of those other objects.

Suppose we consider all the different objects resting on the surface of the Earth. Each one of them is subject to a gravitational attraction between itself and the Earth. Since the Earth's mass is the same in each case, the amount of gravitational pull on each object depends on the mass of the object.

We can measure the gravitational pull on an object on the surface of the Earth by weighing it. The more strongly the Earth pulls it, the "heavier" we say it is. The more weakly Earth pulls it, the "lighter" we say it is. The more mass an object possesses, the more strongly it is pulled to Earth and the heavier it is. The less mass it possesses, the lighter it is.

As long as we restrict ourselves to the surface of the earth, mass and weight are so closely related that we can use either word. However, gravitational attraction decreases with distance. Two objects may be of the same mass, but if one of them is 2630 kilometers (1635 miles) above the Earth's surface, it weighs only half as much as its twin on the surface. Again, astronomical bodies other than the Earth have different intensities of gravitational pull. An object on the surface of the moon weighs only one-sixth as much as an equally massive object on the surface of the Earth.

It is much safer, then, to forget about weight and about "heavy" and "light." Let us, instead, speak of objects as being "more massive" and "less massive."

Can we measure mass in ways other than by weighing objects? Yes, remember that we can compare gravitational intensities.

In 1798 the English scientist Henry Cavendish measured the gravitational pull (an exceedingly tiny one) of a large lead ball on a small lead ball. He knew the gravitational pull of the

Earth on that small lead ball. From the difference in the pulls, he could calculate the difference in mass between the large lead ball and the Earth, making use of Isaac Newton's "Law of Universal Gravitation," which had first been advanced in 1687. Knowing the mass of the large lead ball, he could calculate the mass of the Earth.

It turns out that the Earth has a mass of 6,000,000,000-000,000,000,000,000 kilograms (6,600,000,000,000,000,000,000 tons.)

Once we know the mass of the Earth, we can calculate the mass of other objects in the solar system.

The Earth's gravitational field, for instance, pulls on the moon from a certain distance, and, in response, the moon moves in its orbit at a certain speed and completes its orbit in a certain time. Jupiter has certain satellites at certain distances from itself, and they move at certain speeds, and complete their orbits in certain times. By comparing the distance and period of the moon going around Earth with the distance and period of a satellite going around Jupiter, astronomers can calculate that Jupiter's gravitational field is 318 times as intense as Earth's is. This means that Jupiter is 318 times as massive as Earth.

The Earth is at a certain distance from the sun and moves at a certain speed in response to the sun's gravity and therefore completes its orbit in a certain time. Comparing this with the way in which the moon moves in the grip of Earth's gravity, astronomers can calculate that the sun's mass is equal to 332,-500 times that of the Earth. The sun's mass is 2,000,000,000,-000,000,000,000,000,000,000 kilograms (2,200,000,000,000,000,-000,000,000,000 tons).

Mass is calculated in this manner by making use of "Kepler's Third Law," so-called because it was first worked out by the German astronomer Johann Kepler in 1619. To make use of Kepler's Third Law, however, we must have one object circling another at a definite distance and in a definite time, both of which we can measure.

If a star is isolated in space, with no companions that we can detect, Kepler's Third Law won't work. For binary stars, however, everything is set. If we can measure the average distance between the stars and the time it takes for them to circle about their center of gravity, we can calculate the total mass of the two stars of the binary system by comparing distances and times with distances and times within our own solar system. In Table 22 the total mass of certain binary systems is given.

If the total mass of a binary system is more than twice that of the sun, it is possible that each star of the binary may be more massive than the sun. If the total mass is between 1 and 2 times that of the sun, then one of the stars must be less massive than the sun. For a total mass of less than 1, both stars must be less massive than the sun.

In the case of Alpha Centauri, one of the component stars must be less massive than the sun. Presumably Alpha Centauri B, the less brilliant of the two, is also the less massive.

Actually, one can calculate the mass of each component of a binary by noting the size of the orbit each makes relative to some star that is nearby in the sky and is not part of the system. The more massive star makes a smaller orbit. This system is used, for instance, to calculate the mass of our moon. The moon and Earth circle about the center of gravity of the Earth-moon system, and the ellipse marked out by the Earth's center is only 1/81.3 as wide as that marked out by the moon's center. This means that the Earth's mass is 81.3 times that of the moon.

In Table 23, some binaries are listed in which the mass of each star has been calculated.

As you see from the table, Alpha Centauri A has not only just about the same luminosity as the sun does, but also has almost the same mass. Alpha Centauri B, which is less luminous than the sun, is also less massive.

In fact, as astronomers checked on the mass of different

TABLE 22

Total Mass of Binary Systems

BINARY SYSTEM	TOTAL MASS (SUN'S MASS $= 1$)
Capella	5.3
Castor	3.68
Sirius	3.55
Delta Equulei	3.20
Zeta Sagittarii	3.0
Procyon	2.38
Mizar	2.22
Alpha Centauri	**1.95**
Gamma Virginis	1.74
70 Ophiuchi	1.65
Zeta Herculius	1.6
Eta Ophiuchi	1.5
Delta Cygni	1.4
Alpha Ursa Majoris	1.2
Eta Cassiopeiae	1.18
61 Cygni	1.14
Eta Corona Borealis	1.1
Xi Boötis	1.0
85 Pegasi	0.9
Krüger 60	0.44
Ross 614	0.22

stars, it turned out that the more massive stars were almost always more luminous than the less massive stars. That made it seem as though there was some connection between luminosity and mass.

The connection couldn't be a simple one, because as the masses of more and more stars were determined, it became evident that those masses didn't vary by much. Some stars might be millions of times more luminous than others, yet only a hundred times as massive. Mass varied far less than luminosity did—but, except for certain special cases, always in the same direction.

TABLE 23

Mass of Component Stars of Binary Systems

BINARY SYSTEM	MASS OF A (SUN'S MASS $= 1$)	MASS OF B (SUN'S MASS $= 1$)
Sirius	2.50	1.05
Procyon	1.82	0.56
Alpha Centauri	**1.08**	**0.87**
70 Ophiuchi	0.95	0.70
Krüger 60	0.28	0.16
Ross 614	0.14	0.08

The English astronomer Arthur Stanley Eddington worked on this problem. He argued that a star exerts a gravitational pull on the matter making up its outer layers. The pull gives the star a tendency to shrink. As the star shrinks, the central layers heat up. The heat tends to make the star expand. It takes enormous temperatures in the millions of degrees at the core of the star to make the expansion tendency equal to contraction tendency and keep the star stable.

The more massive a star, the greater its gravitational field and the greater its tendency to contract. The more massive a star, then, the higher the internal temperature required to keep it from contracting. Finally, the more massive a star and the higher the internal temperature, the more light and heat leak out through the surface and the more luminous it is.

Eddington showed that, from this standpoint, the luminosity

would be expected to increase very quickly as the mass increased. His "mass-luminosity law," announced in 1924, fitted what was known about binary stars, and it seemed reasonable to suppose that it fit single stars too. Therefore, when the luminosity of a star is known, and it does not belong to an exceptional class of stars (we'll have something to say about these exceptional classes later in the book), then its mass is known as well.

Eddington's mass-luminosity law sets upper and lower limits on mass. If a star is too massive, the temperature required to keep it from collapsing together under gravitational pull is so high that the star simply blows up in a vast cataclysmic explosion. In fact, stars that are considerably more massive than the sun, but are not too massive to hold together for a time, are likely to explode at some stage in their history.

On the other hand, if a star has less than a certain crucial amount of mass, its temperature at the center never reaches the level required for it to radiate light. It is then not a star at all, but is a dark body that is cold on its surface.

The most massive star yet observed seems to be HD 47129 (the 47,129th star listed in the Henry Draper Catalogue), which seems to have a mass about 140 times that of the sun. Actually, it is a binary consisting of two stars, each about 70 times the mass of the sun. Its massiveness was first pointed out in 1922 by the Canadian astronomer John Stanley Plaskett.

The least massive star we know of is Ross 614B, which is listed in Table 23. At least, this is the least massive object which can be detected by its own light.

Within our solar system, we know many less massive objects that we detect by the sunlight they reflect, even though they are not large enough to develop a temperature that will cause them to glow with their own light. Thus Jupiter, the largest planet of our system, is about 0.001 times the mass of our sun, or 1/80 the mass of Ross 614B. It shines by reflected light only, and if it were not near a star it could not be seen.

Both our sun and the two chief stars of the Alpha Centauri system are comfortable between these limits. Alpha Centauri C is near the lower limit.

Transverse Velocity

Once the distance of the nearer stars was determined, something more could be done with proper motion. These motions are usually measured as seconds of arc per year, but if the distance of a particular star is known, then astronomers can calculate what speed in kilometers per second (or miles per second) would be required to produce the observed proper motion at such a distance.

Actually, all the stars move, *including the sun.*

The stars about us, including the sun, are all part of a huge lens-shaped system of over a hundred billion stars. What we see in the sky as the dim luminous band of the Milky Way is actually a conglomeration of very distant, very faint stars that represent what we see when we look through the lens of stars the long way. The lens-shaped system of stars is called the "galaxy," from a Greek word for "milk." Sometimes it is called the Milky Way galaxy to specify which it is because there are many other galaxies besides our own.

Our sun and all the other stars we have been talking about in this book (except for S Doradus) are in one small section of the galaxy which is 9,200 parsecs (30,000 light-years) from the center (see Figure 4). Our sun and all the other neighborhood stars move in a vast orbit around that center, taking 230 million years to make one complete turn. The stars in our neighborhood turn about the galactic center at a speed of about 220 kilometers (130 miles) per second.

The stars in our neighborhood don't all move at precisely the same speed, however. Some are a little closer to the center than others, some have orbits that are more eccentric than those of others. This means that one star may be gaining a

FIGURE 4
The Galaxy

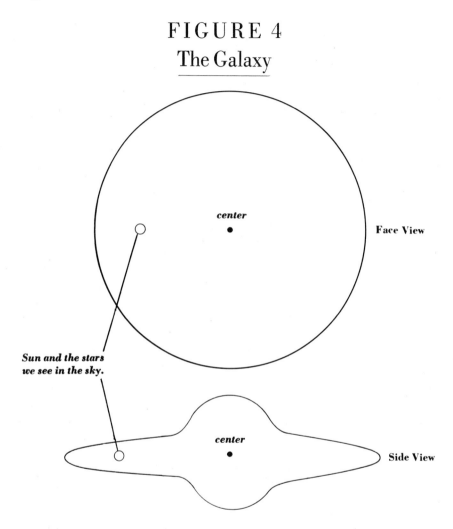

center

Face View

Sun and the stars
we see in the sky.

center

Side View

little on a second at the present moment, and losing ground a little to a third.

It is this gaining or losing that shows up as the proper motion of the stars. The size of the proper motion depends on two things. First, there is the actual speed of the star across our line of vision. This is the "transverse velocity," from Greek words meaning "direction across." Second, there is the distance of the star. If two stars are moving with the same transverse velocity and one is much farther than the other, the farther star seems to be moving much more slowly and to have a much smaller proper motion. Once we determine the distance, however, the transverse velocity is the only unknown left, and it can be easily calculated.

In order to set an actual value on the transverse velocity, the logical thing to do is to pretend that our sun is motionless, and then calculate the velocity relative to ourselves. We can then see how rapidly or how slowly a particular star is gaining on us (or falling behind) as we both race about the galactic center.

In Table 24, the transverse velocities of some stars are given. In every case, a particular star is moving in a particular direction across the sky. The direction, however, would be hard to show without a map of the heavens and we can do without it. Table 24 gives only the velocities.

As you see, Barnard's star, which has the largest proper motion known, is not the star with the greatest transverse velocity. There are at least two stars with a greater transverse velocity.

Here is where the factor of distance comes in. Part of the cause of the high proper motion of Barnard's star rests in the fact that it is so close to us. Barnard's star is less than 6 light-years away, while Kapteyn's star, with a proper motion almost as great, is 13 light-years away.

Alpha Centauri, in respect to transverse velocity as to so many other properites, is in a median position, with a value neither very high nor very low.

Transverse velocity, however, is not all there is to a star's motion, and it doesn't really represent a star's true velocity relative to ourselves. If the sky were a distant solid dome and the various stars were crawling across it all at the same distance from us, then transverse velocity would be all there is— but that's not so. The stars are set in three-dimensional space

TABLE 24

Transverse Velocity of Some Stars

	TRANSVERSE VELOCITY	
STAR	KILOMETERS PER SECOND	MILES PER SECOND
Kapteyn's Star	166	103
Lacaille 9352	118	74
Barnard's Star	90	56
61 Cygni	84	52
Epsilon Indi	77	48
Lacaille 8760	64	40
Lalande 21185	57	35
Wolf 359	54	34
Luyten 789-6	53	33
Groombridge 34	49	30
Luyten 726-8	38	24
Tau Ceti	33	20
Alpha Centauri	**23**	**14.3**
Ross 248	23	14.3
Ross 128	22	13.5
Procyon	20	12.5
Ross 614	18	11.2
Krüger 60	16	10.0
Sirius	16	10.0
Epsilon Eridani	15	9.3
Ross 154	9	5.6

and they can be moving closer to us or farther from us, as well as across our line of vision.

A star may be farther from the galactic center than we are, for instance, but may have a more eccentric orbit and may be cutting across more sharply than we are in order to swoop in closer to the center and it may be approaching us for that reason. Or a star may be moving outward to a greater distance from the galactic center than we ever reach and it may be moving away from us for that reason.

The motion of a star toward us or away from us is called "radial velocity," from a Latin word for a spoke of a wheel. (It is as though we imagined ourselves at the hub of a wheel with the star moving toward us or away from us along the spoke.)

The radial velocity must be known if you wish to know the true velocity of the star.

Suppose two stars are moving at the same velocity, but one is moving directly across our line of vision while the other is moving directly toward us (or directly away from us). The star that is moving directly across our line of vision is changing its position in the sky, and we can detect that as proper motion. The other star, despite its equal speed, is moving directly toward us or away from us and does not change its position in the sky, so we see no proper motion at all.

Most stars move neither directly across our line of vision nor directly toward us or away from us. They move in some in-between direction. We see part of a star's motion as proper motion. The more nearly it slants across our line of vision, the larger the fraction of its motion we see as proper motion. However, unless we know the radial velocity as well as the transverse velocity, we can't figure out what amount of slant there is to a star's motion, and how fast it is really moving relative to ourselves.

How can we detect radial motion?

One way, perhaps, would be to study the apparent brightness of a particular star. As that star moved toward us, it would grow brighter; as it moved away from us, it would grow dimmer. Such changes would be extremely slow, however, and it might take many thousands of years for radial motion to become detectable.

Is there any other way we can detect radial velocity?

Actually, there is. A method for doing so developed quite un-expectedly in the mid-1800s, and to explain how this works we will have to backtrack a little.

6
STARLIGHT

Spectral Lines

In 1666, the English scientist Isaac Newton found that it was possible to pass a beam of sunlight through a triangle of glass called a prism and in that way spread the beam into a length along which different colors would appear in a certain order: red, orange, yellow, green, blue, and violet. Each color would fade into the next with no sharp boundaries.

Sunlight, it seemed, though it appeared white, was a mixture of lights of many different colors. Those colors could be separated out and put back together to form white light again.

Newton called the band of colors a "spectrum," from a Latin word meaning "appearance."

In 1803, the English scientist Thomas Young carried out experiments that showed light to consist of tiny waves, each wave being less than a millionth of a meter long. Light of a particular "wavelength" is bent out of its path ("refracted") in passing through the prism. The shorter the wavelength, the more it is refracted.

White light, such as that from the sun, is a mixture of very many wavelengths and these are sorted out on passing through a prism. In the spectrum, the wavelengths are lined up in order, with the longest wavelengths (red) at one end, the shortest (violet) at the other, and intermediate lengths in between. Different wavelengths affect our eyes in different ways, and these different ways are interpreted in the brain as different colors. It is for that reason that we see the spectrum as a band of colors.

Sunlight does not contain all possible wavelengths of light, however. Some are missing. In the method Newton used to get a spectrum, the separation of the wavelengths was not very efficient. There was so much overlapping that missing wavelengths were obscured by the light of neighboring wavelengths in either direction.

Then, in 1814 the German physicist Joseph von Fraunhofer (FROWN-hoh-fer), passed light through a narrow slit before allowing it to pass through a prism. The result was that he formed the image of the slit in light of every wavelength, and the different wavelengths were much more sharply separated than had been possible before.

Wherever there was a wavelength missing in sunlight, there was an image of a dark slit—a dark line that appeared amid all the bright lines that melted into each other to form a continuous band. Fraunhofer detected nearly six hundred of these "spectral lines," and the most prominent lines he lettered from A to K.

These spectral lines always formed the same pattern in the solar spectrum (the spectrum of sunlight), since it was always the same wavelengths of light that were missing. Astronomers could map these lines, plot their exact position, and determine just which wavelengths were missing.

In 1842 an Austrian scientist, Christian Johann Doppler (DOPE-ler), was working on a problem that seemed to have nothing to do with spectral lines. He was interested in the fact that a particular sound tone changed its pitch if the object producing the tone was moving.

A train whistle, for instance, might have a certain pitch if the train were standing still. If the train were approaching you, the whistle would sound higher-pitched to you, even though to people on the train, moving with the whistle, there would seem to be no change. Again, if the train were moving away from you, the whistle would sound lower-pitched to you, even though to people on the train, moving with the whistle, there again would seem to be no change.

Finally, if the train moved toward you, passed you, and moved away from you, the pitch of the whistle would drop from high to low as it passed.

Doppler tested this out very carefully. He finally decided that the cause of the changing pitch arose out of the fact that sound was composed of waves and that pitch depended on the length of the waves. Short wavelengths of sound produced the effect of high pitch and long wavelengths produced the effect of low pitch. (When you sing the scale from low notes to high notes, you produce sound waves that are shorter and shorter. When you go down the scale, you produce them longer and longer.)

Suppose something that is producing a sound is approaching you. The sound waves that are sent out toward you would be shorter than they would be if that something were standing still. The approaching object catches up slightly to each wavelength before it sends out the next. That is why the pitch is higher for an approaching sound than for that same sound standing still.

If the source of the sound is moving away from you, then each sound wave is sent out from a farther position so that the wave is a little longer than it would be if the sound source were standing still. For that reason, the pitch is lower for a receding sound than for that same sound standing still.

Because of this explanation, the change of pitch with motion is called the "Doppler effect."

A few years later, the French scientist Armand Hippolyte Louis Fizeau (fee-ZOH) pointed out that the Doppler effect could be applied to light, too, since light is a wave phenomenon.

He reasoned that if a source of light were approaching us, all the wavelengths would become shorter. A dark line in the spectrum would therefore move toward the short-wavelength end of the spectrum and there would be a "violet shift."

If a light source were receding from us, all the wavelengths would become longer. A dark line in the spectrum would therefore move toward the long-wavelength end of the spectrum and there would be a "red shift."

With respect to light, this change in wavelength with motion of the source is sometimes called the "Doppler-Fizeau effect."

Although the sun was the first object to yield a spectrum, any other form of light could be made to yield one too. Moonlight, light from the planets, light from ordinary fire, all could yield a spectrum.

What astronomers found themselves most interested in was the spectra produced by stars, stellar spectra. The light from a star could be focused by a telescope and sent through a device called a spectroscope that would produce a spectrum. Of course, stars were very dim compared to the sun and spreading out starlight into a spectrum made the light dimmer still.

At first it was only the very brightest stars that could be made to yield visible spectra. In 1868 the English astronomer William Huggins studied the spectrum of the star Sirius. There were dark lines there too.

Only a few dark lines could be seen in the dim spectrum of Sirius, but they formed the same pattern as some of the most prominent lines in the solar spectrum. The only difference was that the lines in the spectrum of Sirius were all a tiny bit longer in wavelength than the lines in the solar spectrum. There was a small red shift, and Huggins realized that this was so because Sirius was receding from us. It was the first detection of a Doppler-Fizeau effect in connection with stars and meant that, for the first time, the radial velocity of a star had been detected.

Radial Velocity

Could the spectra of dimmer stars be studied also?

In the 1840s photography was invented. Astronomers learned how to focus the light of heavenly objects on a photographic plate and take their pictures. The sun and moon were naturally the first objects photographed, but the stars followed.

In 1850 the American astronomer George Phillips Bond took the photograph of the star Vega, and in 1857 he photographed Mizar. In 1863 Huggins was the first to photograph a stellar spectrum, catching those of Sirius and Capella. These first two spectral photographs were too dim and fuzzy to show any detail, however.

The technique of photography improved with the years, though, and it proved to have a few great advantages over the use of the eye alone.

When light falls on the retina of the eye, it doesn't accumulate. If an object is too dim to see, then staring at the place where it is won't make it visible. It will remain too dim to see. A photographic plate, however, accumulates the chemical changes produced by light. A dim object may not send out enough light to affect the photographic plate visibly, but if you wait, the effects of the light build up and build up. As a result, long exposures enable a photographic plate to take pictures of objects too dim to see without photography. And the photograph is a permanent record, too.

Eventually, photography made it possible to study large numbers of stellar spectra in sufficient detail to detect tiny shifts of the spectral lines and determine the radial velocity.

The study of radial velocity turned out to be far more useful than that of transverse velocity. Transverse velocity can be detected only for the nearest stars, while radial velocity can be detected in any object, however distant. The most distant objects in the universe have had their radial velocity detected, and that has given us important information about the universe as a whole that could have been determined in no other way.

As for the nearer stars, whose transverse velocities are listed in Table 24, the radial velocities have also been determined, and these are listed in Table 25. A positive sign (+) indicates a radial motion away from us; a negative sign (−), a radial motion toward us.

If both the radial velocity and the transverse velocity are known, the two can be combined to work out the actual direction of motion and the true, or "space," velocity can be calculated. This is the actual velocity of the star relative to ourselves in some direction that is neither transverse nor radial, but a combination of the two.

The space velocity of the stars listed in Table 25 as approaching us is given in Table 26; that of the stars listed in Table 25 as receding from us is given in Table 27.

We must not judge from the last few tables that some stars are fast while some are slow. The velocities listed are worked out relative to the sun, so a "slow" star is only one whose velocity nearly matches that of the sun, while a "fast" star is one whose velocity is quite different from that of the sun.

Furthermore, the vision of stars rushing through space at tens and hundreds of kilometers per second should not give rise to thoughts of collisions.

Suppose we imagined the sun to be a little sphere a centimeter (0.4 inches) across. On that scale, Alpha Centauri A would be another little sphere of the same size located 300 kilometers (185 miles) away. Alpha Centauri B would be circling Alpha Centauri A at an average distance of 25 meters (82 feet) and Alpha Centauri C would be about 7 kilometers (4.3 miles) away from the two brighter stars.

In other words, if the sun and its planets, on this small scale, were imagined to be in New York City, the three stars of the Alpha Centauri system would be in or near Worcester, Massachusetts.

What's more, if speeds were reduced in the same way as we imagined the size to be, it would turn out that these small

TABLE 25

Radial Velocity of Some Near Stars

	RADIAL VELOCITY	
STAR	KILOMETERS PER SECOND	MILES PER SECOND
Kapteyn's Star	+242	+150
Luyten 726-8	+ 29	+ 18
Ross 614	+ 24	+ 15
Lacaille 8760	+ 23	+ 14.3
Epsilon Eridani	+ 15	+ 9.3
Groombridge 34	+ 14	+ 8.7
Wolf 359	+ 13	+ 8.1
Lacaille 9352	+ 10	+ 6.2
Procyon	− 3	− 1.9
Ross 154	− 4	− 2.5
Sirius	− 8	− 5.0
Ross 128	− 13	− 8.1
Tau Ceti	− 16	− 10.0
Krüger 60	− 24	− 15.0
Alpha Centauri	**− 25**	**− 15.5**
Epsilon Indi	− 60	− 37
61 Cygni	− 64	− 40
Ross 248	− 81	− 50
Lalande 21185	− 86	− 54
Barnard's Star	−108	− 67

spheres would be moving toward one another at the rate of 2 centimeters (0.8 inches) a day. This gives us an idea of the vast distances separating the stars and of the slowness of their speeds compared to those distances. The chances of collisions are so small, they can be ignored.

At the rate Alpha Centauri is approaching us, it would

TABLE 26

Space Velocity of Some Receding Stars

| STAR | SPACE VELOCITY | |
	KILOMETERS PER SECOND	MILES PER SECOND
Kapteyn's Star	294	183
Epsilon Eridani	212	132
Lacaille 9352	119	74
Lacaille 8760	68	42
Wolf 359	56	35
Groombridge 34	51	32
Luyten 726-8	48	30
Ross 614	30	18.5

take a little over twenty-five thousand years to reach its point of closest approach, three and a half light-years (1.1 parsecs) from us, after which it would skim by us and recede again. It would then be nearly half again as bright as it is now, at magnitude –0.67, almost as bright as Canopus. Of course, Sirius, which is also approaching us, though more slowly, would also be brighter than it is now, so that Alpha Centauri will never be the brightest star in the sky even when it is at its closest to us.

Suppose, though, that we reverse the time scheme. If it is approaching us, then in the past it was farther from us, and if we imagine ourselves moving backward in time, it will be receding from us, and after a hundred thousand years or so it will have doubled its distance and would have sunk to the rank of a second-magnitude star. If any of humanity's early ancestors ever looked at the sky, Alpha Centauri would not have been seen to be a particularly remarkable star.

TABLE 27

Space Velocity of Some Approaching Stars

| | SPACE VELOCITY | |
STAR	KILOMETERS PER SECOND	MILES PER SECOND
Barnard's Star	141	87
61 Cygni	106	66
Lalande 21185	103	64
Epsilon Indi	98	61
Ross 248	84	52
Tau Ceti	37	23
Alpha Centauri	**28**	**17**
Krüger 60	26	16
Ross 128	26	16
Procyon	20	12.5
Sirius	18	11.2
Ross 154	10	6.2

The shift of spectral lines told astronomers more than mere approach and recession.

In 1889 the American astronomer Edward Charles Pickering noticed that the spectral lines of Mizar were double. Of each pair of lines, one was moving toward the red and the other toward the violet. After a while, both simultaneously changed direction, approached each other, crossed, moved away from each other, changed direction again, approached, crossed, and so on.

It would appear that part of the star was receding while another part was approaching. They would then change places so that the part that had been receding was approaching and the part that had been approaching was receding. They would again change places, and so on.

The logical explanation seemed to be that there were two stars, so close together that they could not be seen separately even in the best telescopes. As they circled each other, one would be approaching us while the other was receding. Then, when they had made a half-turn, the one that had been approaching would be receding and vice versa.

Such a two-star system, which can be detected by spectroscope but not by telescope in the ordinary way, is called a "spectroscopic binary." In the case of Mizar, which is a "visual binary"—one that can be seen to be two stars (Mizar A and Mizar B) in a telescope—Mizar A is itself a spectroscopic binary.

The two stars of the spectroscopic binary system of Mizar A are at a distance of 38,000,000 kilometers (24,000,000 miles) from each other, less than the distance separating Mercury and Sun. At the 80-light-year distance of Mizar, this represents a separation of 0.04 seconds of arc, too little to be made out by telescope. The two stars of Mizar A circle each other in a period of 20.5 days.

Spectroscopic binaries are quite common and many have been discovered. Some are much closer together than the two stars of Mizar A. Two stars can be within a million kilometers of each other, almost touching, circling each other in hours.

In the case of the binary system of Alpha Crucis, both components, Alpha Crucis A and Alpha Crucis B, are spectroscopic binaries, so that Alpha Crucis is a four-star system.

In the case of the Castor system, not only are Castor A and Castor B each a spectroscopic binary, but there is a dim, distant companion, Castor C, which is *also* a spectroscopic binary. Castor is thus a six-star system.

The spectroscope cannot tell us what is *not* a spectroscopic binary. We can tell, by ordinary telescopic inspection, that Alpha Centauri is a three-star system. Are any of the three stars spectroscopic binaries? Alpha Centauri A, B, and C do not seem to have close companions, and a three-star system is what it probably is, but we can't be entirely sure.

Spectral Classes

Once stellar spectra began to be studied, it was noticed that they were not all alike. Many differed from that of the sun, and from each other, too. In 1867 the Italian astronomer Pietro Angelo Secchi (SAY-kee) suggested that the spectra be divided into four classes based on their differences in appearance— on the number and kinds of lines present, for instance.

As more and more spectra were studied in more and more detail, it quickly turned out that four classes were not enough to describe the situation. In the 1890s, largely through the work of the American astronomer Annie Jump Cannon, a more detailed system was established in which the classes were distinguished by letters of the alphabet.

It turned out that if the different kinds of spectra were placed in what seemed a natural kind of order—where certain lines grew steadily weaker and less prominent as one went from class to class, while others grew stronger and more prominent —then the leters of the Cannon system would be arranged as follows:

O, B, A, F, G, K, M, R, N, S

Of these O, R, N, and S are very rare types. Generally, the stars we deal with belong to the classes B, A, F, G, K, and M, usually listed in that order.

In the transition from one spectral class to the next, various subclasses can be detected and it has become customary to subdivide each class into ten subclasses numbered from 0 to 9.

The typical G spectrum might be considered G0, for instance. Then one could progress through spectra that showed stronger and stronger touches of the next spectral class; through G1, G2, until finally G9 was reached. A G9 spectrum would be nearly K, and the next stage would, indeed, be Ko. The spectral classification of the bright stars is given in Table 28; and of the near stars in Table 29.

Temperature

What is the meaning of the various spectral classes? Why are some spectra different from others? As far back as 1859, two German scientists, Robert Wilhelm Bunsen and Gustav Robert Kirchhoff, had shown that the lines in spectra were particular wavelengths given out or absorbed by certain kinds of atoms.

Each kind of atom gave out or absorbed a particular pattern of wavelengths. No two different kinds of atoms gave out or absorbed the same wavelength.

This meant that if one were to heat any substance until it gave out light that could be spread out into a spectrum, one could tell from the lines the various different kinds of atoms (the various elements) that were present in the substance. This was the beginning of spectroscopic analysis. In 1859 and 1860 Bunsen and Kirchhoff were able to discover two new elements, cesium and rubidium, by heating certain minerals and locating spectral lines that did not belong to any known element.

Might this not be done for the sun and the stars? Would not the lines in their spectra indicate the presence of certain elements within them? In 1862, for instance, the Swedish physicist Anders Jonas Angström (ONG-strom) was able to demonstrate the presence of the element hydrogen in the sun, from the lines of its spectrum.

In 1868 the French astronomer Pierre Jules César Janssen (zhahn-SEN) detected lines in the solar spectrum that did not belong to any known element. He sent a report on this to the English astronomer Joseph Norman Lockyer, an expert on spectra. Lockyer felt it was a new element, which he called helium from the Greek word for "sun." (It was not until nearly thirty years later that helium was discovered on Earth.)

Might it be, then, that different stars were composed of

TABLE 28

Spectral Classification of Some Bright Stars

STAR	SPECTRAL CLASSIFICATION
Beta Centauri	B1
Alpha Crucis	B1
Spica	B2
Achernar	B5
Rigel	B8
Regulus	B8
Sirius	A0
Vega	A0
Deneb	A2
Fomalhaut	A3
Altair	A5
Canopus	F0
Procyon	F5
Capella	G0
Alpha Centauri	**G2**
Arcturus	K0
Pollux	K0
Aldebaran	K5
Antares	M1
Betelgeuse	M2

different elements and that stars with one sort of makeup would be brighter than others?

Lockyer thought otherwise. He felt that stars had similar makeups, by and large. What made the difference in spectra, he felt, was temperature. Although the various lines signified various elements, the lines might change their patterns as the elements were heated to different temperatures.

TABLE 29

Spectral Classification of the Nearest Stars

STAR	SPECTRAL CLASSIFICATION
Sirius A	A1
Sirius B	A5
Procyon A	F5
Alpha Centauri A	**G2**
Tau-Ceti	G8
Epsilon Eridani	K2
Epsilon Indi	K5
61 Cygni A	K5
Alpha Centauri B	**K5**
61 Cygni B	K7
Groombridge 34A	M1
Lalande 21185	M2
Sigma 2398A	M3
Sigma 2398B	M4
Ross 128	M5
Ross 154	M5
Barnard's Star	M5
Alpha Centauri C	**M5**
Wolf 359	M6
Luyten 726-8A	M6
Luyten 726-8B	M6
Ross 248	M6
Luyten 789-6	M6
Groombridge 34B	M6

Lockyer's suggestion held up. In the laboratory, as substances were heated more and more hotly their spectras did change, and these changes led astronomers to match up the various spectral classes with various surface temperatures of the stars.

Then, too, in 1893 the German scientist Wilhelm Wien (VEEN) showed how the entire pattern of the spectrum changed with temperature, how the peak radiation was located in different parts of the spectrum as the temperature rose. That, too, helped determine the surface temperatures of stars.

The temperatures associated with the various spectral classes are given in Table 30, both in Celsius degrees (in which the freezing point of water is at 0° and the boiling point at 100°) and in Fahrenheit degrees (where the corresponding figures are 32 ° for the freezing point and 212 ° for the boiling point).

TABLE 30

Temperatures of the Spectral Classes

| | SURFACE TEMPERATURE OF THE STARS | |
SPECTRAL CLASS	° CELSIUS	° FAHRENHEIT
05	35,000	60,000
B0	22,000	40,000
B5	14,000	25,000
A0	11,000	20,000
A5	8,300	15,000
F0	7,200	13,000
F5	6,700	12,000
G0	6,100	11,000
G5	5,600	10,000
K0	5,000	9,000
K5	4,500	8,000
M0	3,900	7,000
M5	2,800	5,000

Alpha Centauri A is a moderately hot star, then, with a temperature of just under 6,000° C, and in this it is exactly like our sun, which also belongs to the G2 spectral class.

Alpha Centauri B is a cooler star with a surface temperature of only 4,400° C, and Alpha Centauri C is cooler still, with a surface temperature of only 3,000° C.

7
SIZE
AND
CHANGE

Red Giants and White Dwarfs

In general the hotter a star is, the brighter it is. It's no surprise, therefore, that so many of the bright stars in the sky are hotter than the sun is, or that so many of the dim stars we see are cooler than the sun is.

What *is* surprising is that some stars are cool and yet are very bright. The two prime examples of this are Antares and Betelgeuse. Both are in spectral class M and are therefore possessed of a surface temperature of only 3,000° C or so and, what's more, neither one is particularly close to us—and yet each is among the brightest stars in the sky.

In 1905 a Danish astronomer, Ejnar Hertzsprung, reasoned that a cool star must have a dim surface, but if it had a very large surface, the dimness of each bit would add up to a great *total* brightness. In other words, a bright star that was cool and red had to be a very large star indeed in order to be bright.

Hertzsprung published this idea in a journal of photography and astronomers didn't notice it. Then, in 1914, the American astronomer Henry Norris Russell had the same idea independently, and this time the idea stuck and both astronomers are usually given credit.

The Hertzsprung-Russell reasoning led to the concept of "red

giants" among the stars. When attempts were made to calculate how large these red giants would have to be in order to be
as bright as they were despite their low surface temperature,
the results seemed almost unbelievable. In 1920, however, the
German-American physicist Albert Abraham Michelson (MY-
kul-sun) was able to check the matter directly.

To do this, he made use of an instrument he had invented
twenty years earlier, an instrument he called an interferometer. It was capable of measuring, with great delicacy, the
manner in which two trains of light waves, which were not
quite parallel to each other, interfered with each other. When
such trains of light waves were not quite parallel, the waves
as they merged sometimes reinforced each other and sometimes canceled each other, setting up patterns of alternate
light and dark. From the details of such an interference pattern, the exact angle at which the light waves met could be
deduced.

Such an instrument can be applied to the stars. A star is so
small, as seen from Earth, that it is virtually a dot of light. The
light rays coming from the two opposite edges of so tiny a
dot seem to come to us almost from the same direction, and
are therefore almost parallel—almost, *but not quite*. The
light rays come from very slightly different directions as they
reach us from opposite sides of a star; they converge just a
tiny bit, enough to produce an interference pattern if the interferometer is large enough.

Michelson made use of a twenty-foot interferometer, the
largest he had constructed up to that time. He attached it to
the new 100-inch telescope that had just been put into use at
Mount Wilson in California, and which was then the largest
telescope in the world. He turned this instrument on the star
Betelgeuse.

From the nature of the interference pattern, Michelson could
determine the apparent diameter of Betelgeuse. It turned out
to be 0.045 seconds of arc. This is a very small width, for it

would take 41,500 little dots of reddish light just like Betel-geuse, placed side by side, to stretch across the width of the moon.

Yet, Betelgeuse has the largest apparent diameter of any star. Any star that has a true size greater than Betelgeuse is so far away as to have a smaller apparent size. Then, too, any star that is closer than Betelgeuse is so much smaller in true size that its apparent size never comes up to the Betelgeuse mark.

To be even 0.045 seconds in diameter, tiny though that angle is, at the vast distance of Betelgeuse, the star must have an enormous real diameter. In fact, it turns out that the diameter of Betelgeuse is at least 800 times that of the sun.

The interferometer result showed that the reasoning of Hertzsprung and Russell was correct and there really were red giant stars, with Betelgeuse, large as it is, not the largest in actual size. In Table 31, the diameters of some of the giant stars are given.

The large red giants would seem to be impressive objects indeed. Imagine Betelgeuse in place of our sun. We could not see it from Earth, because there would be no Earth. The place where Earth would be, if it existed, would be *within* Betelgeuse. The diameter of Betelgeuse is so large that, if substituted for the sun, it would include the orbits of Mercury, Venus, Earth, and Mars.

Epsilon Aurigae B would do better than that. It would swal-low up the orbit of Saturn as well, and its surface would be nearly at the orbit of Uranus. What's more, that super-giant, Epsilon Aurigae B, is part of a binary system, with the other star, Epsilon Aurigae A, considerably smaller but still large enough to swallow up the orbit of Mars. What a view those stars must be from not-too-near by.

Another way of emphasizing the size of the red giants is to imagine a hollow sphere the size of Beta Pegasi, which is only a moderate-size giant. It would still be large enough to hold

TABLE 31

Giant Stars

| | DIAMETER | | |
STAR	MILLIONS OF KILOMETERS	MILLIONS OF MILES	SUN = 1
Epsilon Aurigae B	2,800	1,700	2,000
VV Cephei A	1,700	1,200	1,400
Betelgeuse	700	435	500
Mira (Omicron Ceti)	550	350	400
Antares	550	350	400
Xi Aurigae A	420	260	300
Epsilon Aurigae A	280	170	200
Beta Pegasi	150	95	110
Aldebaran	61	38	44
Arcturus	37	23	27

1,300,000 objects the size of our sun. A hollow sphere the size of Betelgeuse would hold nearly 43,000,000 objects the size of our sun, and one the size of Epsilon Aurigae B would hold 8,000,000,000 suns.

And yet, for all that, the red giants are perhaps not as impressive as they seem from their size alone. They are more massive than the sun, but not very much more massive. Betelgeuse might take up 43,000,000 times as much space as the sun does, but the red giant is only about 20 times as massive as the sun; it contains only 20 times as much matter.

If the mass of Betelgeuse (not so very great) is spread over the enormous volume taken up by Betelgeuse, that mass must be spread very, very thin.

The sun's average density is 1.41 grams per cubic centimeter, but Betelgeuse's average density is a ten millionth of that. If the sun were only as dense, on the average, as Betelgeuse is, it would have a mass of not more than 1/30 that of the Earth, and only 2.7 times that of the moon.

Epsilon Aurigae B would be far less dense still. The red giants are thin collections of gas that stretch out over enormous distances and glow red-hot, but on an earthly scale they are almost vacuums. The average density of Epsilon Aurigae B is only a thousandth that of Earth's atmosphere, and in its outer regions the density is far less even than that. (Like all stars, red giants get denser as one approaches their center, and in the core they can get very dense indeed. This must be true of all stars, since only in a very dense core can the nuclear conflagration that powers them be ignited.)

The reverse of the case of the red giants arose in connection with Sirius B. That was known to be a very dim star with a magnitude of 10 and a luminosity only 1/130 that of our sun. It was taken for granted that it had to be both small and cool to deliver only 1/130 as much light as our sun.

In 1915, however, the American astronomer Walter Sydney Adams succeeded in taking the spectrum of Sirius B, and found it to be just as hot as Sirius A and, therefore, considerably hotter than our sun.

Yet if Sirius B were that hot, its surface should blaze with white light, and the only way of explaining its dimness was to suppose that it had very little surface.

Sirius B had to have so little surface as to be a dwarf star, far smaller than, till then, anyone had a notion a star could be. Because of its white-hot temperature, it was called a "white dwarf." To account for its dimness, its diameter had to be only 30,000 kilometers (19,000 miles) across, so that it was about as large as a medium-sized planet, and took up only about 13 times as much volume as the Earth. Sirius B has only 1/100 the volume of the large planet, Jupiter.

In the relatively small volume of Sirius B, however, is packed just as much mass as in the sun—as we can tell from the strength of its gravitational pull on Sirius A. If red giants have very low densities, white dwarfs have very high ones. The average density of Sirius B is about 90,000 times that of the sun, or 6,000 times that of platinum.

This would have seemed ridiculous only a couple of decades earlier, but by 1915 it had been discovered that atoms were made up of still smaller "subatomic particles," with almost all the mass concentrated in a very tiny "atomic nucleus" at the center of the atom. In white dwarfs, then, matter didn't exist as ordinary atoms, but as a chaotic mixture of subatomic particles squeezed much more closely together than they are in atoms as we know them.

There are white dwarfs smaller and denser than Sirius B, and in recent years astronomers have discovered new types of stars that are much smaller even than white dwarfs and correspondingly more dense. These are "neutron stars" in which the subatomic particles are practically in contact, and in which the mass of a star like our sun would be compacted into a tiny body only a dozen kilometers across.

The Main Sequence

Both giants and dwarfs, however, are unusual stars and are of rather rare occurrence. The various dwarfs may make up about 8 percent of the stars in the sky, and the various giants about 1 percent. The remaining 90 percent or more of all the stars in the sky are rather sunlike. Some are a little bigger, brighter, and less dense than the sun and some are a little smaller, dimmer, and more dense, but they are not startlingly brighter or dimmer; they are not enormous giants or tiny dwarfs.

These sunlike stars can be arranged according to temperature from very hot to quite cool, as determined by their spectral class. Their other properties then form a sequence too; that is,

they change in a smooth and unsurprising way as one pro-
gresses from hot to cold. Going down the sequence, stars
growing steadily less massive, dimmer, cooler, denser.

Because this sequence includes the vast majority of the
stars, it is called "the main sequence."

Table 32 gives some of the properties of the main-sequence
stars. The table would make it appear that Class-G stars, to
which the sun and Alpha Centauri A belong, are rather smaller
than average. The largest main-sequence stars are about 32
times as massive and about 15 times as wide as the sun, while
the sun is, in turn, only about 4 times as massive as the smallest main-sequence stars and only about 2.5 times as wide.

This would be so if the various spectral classes each contained the same number of stars. This is not so, however. As
in every group of astronomical bodies, the smaller bodies are
more numerous than the larger ones. In Table 33 the percen-
tage of main-sequence stars in each spectral class is given,
together with the total number of each in our galaxy. (Our
galaxy contains about 135,000,000,000 stars altogether, of which
122,000,000,000 are main-sequence, 12,000,000,000 are dwarfs,
and 1,000,000,000 are giants.)

As you see from Table 33, about 87 percent of the stars are
in spectral classes K and M and are, therefore, distinctly
smaller, cooler, and dimmer than our sun. Only about 4.1 percent of the stars are distinctly larger, hotter, and brighter than
our sun. From this standpoint our sun and Alpha Centauri A
are well above average in size.

Suppose that we consider next some of the familiar stars in
the sky, as in Table 34, and see what their diameters might be
compared to the sun.

As you see, Alpha Centauri C is very small for a main-
sequence star. It has only about 0.22 times the mass of the sun
and only 0.25 times its diameter. Nevertheless, it is not the
smallest star known, and included in Table 34 is a star known
to be smaller than Alpha Centauri C. That is Luyten 726-8 B.

TABLE 32

The Main-Sequence Stars

SPECTRAL CLASS	AVERAGE MASS (SUN = 1)	AVERAGE DENSITY (SUN = 1)	AVERAGE DIAMETER		
			KILOMETERS	MILES	SUN = 1
05	32	0.01	28,000,000	17,000,000	20
B0	16	0.03	12,500,000	7,800,000	9
B5	6	0.10	5,500,000	3,500,000	4
A0	3	0.25	3,000,000	1,900,000	2.2
A5	2	0.4	2,400,000	1,500,000	1.7
F0	1.75	0.5	2,100,000	1,300,000	1.5
F5	1.25	0.7	1,700,000	1,100,000	1.25
G0	1.06	1.0	1,450,000	900,000	1.05
G5	0.92	1.3	1,250,000	800,000	0.92
K0	0.80	1.6	1,150,000	720,000	0.83
K5	0.69	2.4	970,000	600,000	0.70
M0	0.48	3.2	830,000	520,000	0.60
M5	0.20	15	350,000	220,000	0.25

TABLE 33

Spectral Class Frequency

SPECTRAL CLASS	PERCENTAGE OF STARS	NUMBER OF STARS IN THE GALAXY
O	0.00002	20,000
B	0.1	100,000,000
A	1	1,200,000,000
F	3	3,700,000,000
G	9	11,000,000,000
K	14	17,000,000,000
M	73	89,000,000,000

TABLE 34

Diameters of Stars

STAR	KILOMETERS	DIAMETER MILES	SUN = 1
Beta Centauri	14,000,000	8,650,000	10
Achernar	11,000,000	6,900,000	8
Spica	9,600,000	6,000,000	7
Regulus	6,000,000	3,700,000	4.3
Procyon	2,900,000	1,800,000	2.1
Altair	2,630,000	1,650,000	1.9
Sirius A	2,500,000	1,550,000	1.8
Fomalhaut	2,500,000	1,550,000	1.8
Capella	1,400,000	873,000	1.01
Alpha Centauri A	**1,390,000**	**865,000**	**1.00**
Tau Ceti	1,170,000	725,000	0.84
Epsilon Eridani	1,060,000	660,000	0.76
61 Cygni A	973,000	605,000	0.70
Alpha Centauri B	**973,000**	**605,000**	**0.70**
61 Cygni B	903,000	562,000	0.65
Barnard's Star	360,000	220,000	0.25
Alpha Centauri C	**360,000**	**220,000**	**0.25**
Luyten 726-8 B	180,000	111,500	0.13
Ross 614 B	120,000	75,000	0.08

It is interesting to compare these small stars, not with the sun but with Jupiter, the largest planet of the solar system. We can see this comparison in Table 35.

As you see, although Alpha Centauri C, Luyten 726-8 B, and Ross 614 B are considerably more massive than Jupiter, they are also considerably denser and are therefore not very much more sizable.

The red dwarfs are near the lower limit of size and brightness for a star. A body can't be much smaller than Ross

614 B without becoming unable to shine. Again, Jupiter is near the upper limit of size for a planet. A body can't be much larger than Jupiter without becoming able to shine. Somewhere there is a borderline region between planet and star and it is at masses between those of Jupiter and Ross 614 B.

Nuclear Energy

What keeps a star shining?

This question did not bother astronomers until the 1840s. Before that time, it was assumed that the stars, and the sun among them, simply shone because that was their property. The stars shone in the way that gold was yellow. The yellowness of gold didn't diminish with time; it didn't get used up So it seemed to be with the shining of the stars.

The turning point came in the 1840s, when the "law of conservation of energy" was worked out by several scientists, including the German scientist Hermann Ludwig Ferdinand von Helmholtz. By the law of conservation of energy, energy could be neither created nor destroyed; it could only change its form.

TABLE 35
Small Stars and Giant Planets

OBJECT	MASS (JUPITER = 1)	DIAMETER (JUPITER = 1)
Alpha Centauri C	260	2.4
Luyten 726-8 B	135	1.3
Ross 614 B	80	0.8
Jupiter	1	1.0

To Helmholtz that raised the question of sunlight. Light is a form of energy, and the sun has been radiating light in all directions in huge quantities for uncounted millions of years. The energy had to come from somewhere; it couldn't be created out of nothing.

In 1854 Helmholtz decided that the only possible source of

energy was gravitational contraction. The sun was slowly contracting; all parts of itself were slowly falling toward the center. The energy of motion of this fall was converted into light and was radiated outward in all directions.

This would mean that in the past the sun was more voluminous than it is now. In fact, in order to supply the amount of energy the sun has radiated away in the last 25 million years, the sun would have had to have a diameter of 300,000,000 kilometers (186,000,000 miles) to begin with and to have contracted to its present diameter of 1,400,000 kilometers (864,000 miles) in that time.

It seemed, then, by Helmholtz's reasoning that the sun must have been what we would now call a red giant about 25 million years ago and that its volume then extended to the Earth's orbit. That, in turn, meant that the Earth could not have existed before that, and could be only 25 million years old.

This seemed wrong to geologists who studied the Earth's crust and were sure that it was much older than 25 million years. It also seemed wrong to biologists who studied evolution and were sure that it had taken more than 25 million years for modern life to develop.

The only way out of the dilemma was to find a new source of energy, one that was greater than any known in Helmholtz's time, upon which the sun (and other stars) might be drawing.

This came to pass. In the 1890s radioactivity was discovered, and this led to the realization that the atom has a structure. At its very center is a tiny "atomic nucleus" only one hundred thousandth the diameter of the atom itself, yet in that very compact nucleus almost all the mass of the atom is squeezed. Around it, in the outskirts of the atom, are present one or more light particles called electrons which contain at most about 1/1800 of the mass of the atom.

Chemical changes take place when electrons shift from one atom to another, and the result of such shifts is that chemical energy is absorbed or given off. The energy of living things, including the energy we develop in our own bodies, is such chemical energy. The light and heat of a bonfire, the way in which burning gasoline makes a car go, or the way in which exploding dynamite shatters rock are all examples of chemical energy being converted into other forms of energy.

The atomic nucleus is made up of still smaller particles, protons and neutrons. Like electrons, these nuclear particles can shift, break away, combine, and so on. The result is that nuclear energy is absorbed or given off in quantities generally much greater, for a given weight of substance, than is the case with chemical energy.

A nuclear bomb is an example of the conversion of nuclear energy into other forms.

Once it was understood that nuclear energy existed, it could be seen quickly that somehow this had to be the source of sunlight. But what was it that went on inside the sun to release the nuclear energy?

Since the sun is mostly hydrogen, the source must be in nuclear reactions involving the hydrogen nucleus. Nothing else is common enough in the sun to account for all the energy it has given off, not in just a few millions of years, but in thousands of millions of years. There is evidence to indicate that the sun has been shining for about five billion years in much the same way it is shining now.

In 1938 the German-American physicist Hans Albrecht Bethe (BAY-tuh) made use of the knowledge gathered in the previous forty years concerning atomic nuclei to show that the energy must arise from the combination or "fusion" of four hydrogen nuclei to form a helium nucleus.

In order to keep the sun shining at its present rate, about 590 million metric tons of hydrogen must be converted into 585.8 million metric tons of helium *every second!* (The missing 4.2 million metric tons is converted into sunlight.) This may make it seem that the sun is losing weight at an alarming rate, but actually there is so much hydrogen in the sun altogether that the loss can go on for billions of years in its present fashion without seriously changing the situation.

Stellar Evolution

Astronomers have now worked out what they think the progressive changes in a star must be like—the details of "stellar evolution."

Before stars are born, there are large and voluminous collections of thin dust and gas—mostly hydrogen. Slowly, the dust and gas form a nebula, which swirls and comes together under the pull of its own gravity. The nebula becomes smaller and denser, and at its center it becomes denser still.

As the nebula condenses, the center becomes not only denser and denser but hotter and hotter, as the energy of falling inward is turned to heat (as Helmholtz had suggested). The hydrogen nuclei smash together at greater and greater speeds, and with more and more energy.

If the nebula is small to begin with, it could end up as a compact body no more massive than the planet Jupiter. In that case, the center may be very dense and hot, but it is not sufficiently dense and hot to cause the hydrogen atoms to fuse into helium. To bring about such fusion, temperatures of millions of degrees must be attained. For objects the size of Jupiter or less, there is never any chance of "nuclear ignition" at the center and the body does not shine by its own light. However hot the center may be, the surface is cold and dark.

If the nebula is large enough to end up as a compact body at least 40 times as massive as Jupiter, then the density and temperature at the center reach the point of ignition. Enough energy is released, in that case, to heat up the rest of the body so that the object begins to shine and is a star.

Stars merely a few dozen or even a couple of hundred times as massive as Jupiter are still so small that even though they are large enough to reach the point of nuclear ignition, their temperatures get only high enough to raise their surface to

3000° C so that they are merely red hot. Alpha Centauri C, 230 times as massive as Jupiter, is an example of this.

A larger nebula would condense to a body that was more massive and could therefore reach higher densities and temperatures at the center, produce more rapid nuclear fusion, and attain higher temperatures.

Condensing nebulae, once they have condensed far enough to ignite, enter the main sequence. The exact position at which they enter depends on the mass of the condensing body. A small body like Alpha Centauri C becomes a Class M star. More and more massive bodies enter at Class K, like Alpha Centauri B, or at Class G, like Alpha Centauri A and our sun. Still larger masses enter as Class A, B, or even O.

Once a star is on the main sequence, it stays there and delivers energy at a pretty constant rate, until its hydrogen supply starts to run low. When that happens, things begin to change. The center of the star has been getting steadily hotter as it has grown older, and if the star is large enough the central temperatures reach the point where other kinds of nuclear reactions than that of hydrogen fusing to helium can take place.

The other kinds of nuclear reactions do not make as much energy available as hydrogen fusion does, and the star begins to change its appearance radically. To begin with, it begins to expand and, in doing so, its surface cools down and becomes no more than red hot. The star expands into a red giant, in other words. The more massive the star was to begin with, the more huge will be the red giant into which it turns.

After the red giant stage, the star shrinks again into a white dwarf or an even more compact star. Before the shrinkage, or during it, a particularly large star may explode very violently and blow most of its mass into space.

Once a star runs low on its hydrogen supply and begins to expand, it has "left the main sequence." Compared to the time it stays on the main sequence, the time that passes after it leaves and before shrinkage to a white dwarf (with or without explosion) is quite short. Similarly, the time it takes for a nebula to condense to the point where a star enters the main sequence is quite short.

The major portion of the lifetime of a star is spent on the main sequence. That is why some 90 percent of the stars in existence have already reached the main sequence and have not yet left it.

But just how long does a star remain on the main sequence?

Naturally, it depends on the size of the star, but perhaps not in the way one might expect. A large star has a larger supply of hydrogen than a small star does, so you might expect that a large star will have a chance to burn longer and stay on the main sequence longer than a small star does—but this is not so. The fact of the matter is quite the other way around.

You see, the larger a star is, the hotter its center must be to keep that star expanded against the contracting pull of gravity. And the hotter it must be, the faster hydrogen must fuse and the more rapid the rate at which hydrogen must disappear. The rate at which hydrogen must disappear increases much faster than the mass does. If one star is twice the mass of another, the larger star uses up hydrogen much more than twice as rapidly as the other, so that the larger star actually consumes its fuel first.

Therefore, the larger the star, the shorter its main-sequence lifetime. In Table 36 an estimate is given for the lifetime on the main sequence for stars of different spectral classes. In Table 37, an estimate of the lifetime on the main sequence is given for certain specific stars.

As you can see from Tables 36 and 37, the lifetime of the very massive stars is short indeed. That is one of the reasons why there are so few massive stars on the main sequence— they vanish so quickly. The various red giants and white dwarfs are, probably, most of them the dying remains of stars considerably more massive than the sun. Stars considerably dimmer than the sun haven't had time to die yet in the course of the existence of the universe (which may be some 25 billion years old).

Working backward, the ordinary bright stars that fill our sky, and which we think of first when we think of stars, can't be very old. If they were, they would already have left the main sequence and would be red giants or white dwarfs. In the days of the dinosaurs, Spica, Sirius, Rigel, Regulus, Vega and other such stars simply weren't in the sky. They hadn't formed yet. And a few million years from now, they'll be gone.

Sirius A, when it first formed, probably circled Sirius B, which was formed at the same time and which was much

TABLE 36

Life-Span on the Main Sequence
(spectral classes)

SPECTRAL CLASS	LUMINOSITY (SUN = 1)	LIFE-SPAN ON THE MAIN SEQUENCE (BILLIONS OF YEARS)
O	6,000,000	less than 0.001
B0	6,000	0.01
B5	600	0.1
A0	60	0.5
A5	20	1.0
F0	6	2.0
F5	3	4.0
G0	1.3	10
G5	0.8	15
K0	0.4	20
K5	0.1	30
M0	0.02	75
M5	0.001	200

TABLE 37

Life-Span on the Main Sequence
(individual stars)

STAR	LIFE-SPAN ON THE MAIN SEQUENCE (BILLIONS OF YEARS)
Beta Centauri	0.01
Rigel	0.4
Sirius A	0.5
Altair	1.0
Canopus	2.0
Procyon A	4.0
Capella	10
Alpha Centauri A	**12**
Sun	12
Tau Ceti	18
Alpha Centauri B	**30**
61 Cygni A	30
61 Cygni B	40
Barnard's Star	200
Alpha Centauri C	**200**

more massive than Sirius A to begin with. Millions of years ago Sirius B came to the end of its stay on the main sequence, exploded, blew most of its substance into space, and what was left, less massive than Sirius A, shrank into a white dwarf.

Our sun is a star of intermediate life expectancy, since it is a star of intermediate mass and luminosity. Its lifetime on the main sequence is about 12 billion years. It has been shining now for about 5 billion years, so it is still on the young side of middle age—though since it will grow very slowly warmer, the old side won't be as comfortable as the young side was.

Alpha Centauri A has a lifetime on the main sequence equal to that of the sun, but we can't be certain how much of that lifetime has been used up. Our knowledge of the sun's age is derived largely from data concerning the Earth, the moon, and meteorites. If Alpha Centauri A (concerning which we do not have similar data) was born before the sun was, it will leave the main sequence and swell into a not-very-large red giant while our sun is still burning away as usual. If Alpha Centauri A was born after our sun, then it is we who will go first.

One thing we can be certain of is that the swelling to giant and shrinking to dwarf will be accomplished in the case of the sun, of Alpha Centauri, and of any of the other stars of intermediate or small mass, without catastrophic explosion. The great explosions are characteristic of the large, massive, short-lived stars.

If we can't be sure whether the sun and Alpha Centauri A were formed at the same time or not, and if not, which was formed first, we can at least be reasonably sure that Alpha Centauri A, Alpha Centauri B, and Alpha Centauri C were all formed at the same time out of one swirling nebula that tore into three unequal parts before completing its condensation.

Alpha Centauri A, having been born of the most massive fragment, may have condensed a bit more rapidly than the other two, and Alpha Centauri C a bit less rapidly than the other two. The difference in rate, however, was probably small compared to the total lifetime, and we might as well say that all three members of the Alpha Centauri system are about the same age.

They will not all live out the same lifetimes on the main sequence, however. When Alpha Centauri A leaves the main sequence, Alpha Centauri B will have lived out only 2/5 of its lifetime, and Alpha Centauri C only 1/12 of its lifetime. A hundred billion years after the sun and Alpha Centauri A are white dwarfs, slowly, slowly cooling to black dwarfs, Alpha Centauri C will still be gleaming its dull red, much as it is today, with billions of years of life still ahead of it.

8

LIFE AMONG THE STARS

The Suitable Stars

Throughout this book, so far, we have had a picture of a vast universe with numerous stars separated from one another by enormous distances. In all this vastness, is there such a thing as life anywhere but in the one place we know life to exist— right here on Earth?

Of course, we might ask what we mean by life.

We know our own kind only. All life on Earth is very similar chemically. All of it is based on very large, very complex, very delicate molecules of which the chief belong to groups called proteins and nucleic acids. These molecules are very similar in all forms of life from the most complex to the most simple, and in all cases they are either dissolved in, or very intimately associated with, water.

Is this the only kind of life that can possibly exist? Might some forms of life be based on other types of complex molecules? The complex molecules in our kind of life are built of intricate rings and chains of carbon atoms, with other kinds of atoms (chiefly hydrogen, nitrogen, and oxygen) attached here and there. Might other forms of life not use carbon atoms at all? Might some forms of life be based on simple molecules or involve some liquid other than water? Might there be some forms of life so strange as to defy description?

We can talk about such strange forms of life and speculate about it, but there is no evidence for any of it. We haven't received the slightest scrap of information from anywhere in the universe that would give us the slightest cause to think that strange forms of life *not* based on proteins, nucleic acids, and water are possible.

Until such evidence does show up, we have no choice but to confine the discussion to life only as we know it. We have to ask if life similar to our own in basic chemistry exists anywhere in the universe. Of course, we have no evidence for that either, but at least we know that it exists here on Earth, so we don't draw a complete blank there.

Even though we don't have direct evidence for our kind of life (let's call it just "life" for short) elsewhere, we can consider the kind of conditions we would need for it (based on what we know of ourselves and our own world) and see whether we can honestly expect life to exist elsewhere than on Earth.

For instance, life must have a constant supply of energy to keep those complicated molecules in being. Without energy, those molecules can't be formed, and any that already exist break down, so that life would cease to be.

The only place we know of where life can be assured of a copious supply of energy over a period of billions of years is in the neighborhood of a star.

That means there are a lot of places where life can be assured of an energy supply. The star system to which our own sun belongs, the Milky Way galaxy, includes perhaps 135,000,-000,000 stars. In the universe, as far as can be reached by our most advanced instruments, there may be as many as 100,-000,000,000 other galaxies, each with its billions of stars.

Suppose we just consider our own galaxy. If we conclude that life might exist in a certain number of places in that galaxy, we need only multiply that number by a hundred billion or so to find out how many places there are in the entire observable universe.

Not every star is a good neighborhood for life, however. Once a star leaves the main sequence, its swellings, shrinkings, and possible explosions are sure to wipe out any life that exists in its vicinity. We must restrict ourselves, then, to the main-sequence stars. That still leaves us with 90 percent of all the stars there are in the galaxy, or about 122,000,000,000 of them.

But what about main-sequence stars? Are some of them more suitable for life than others?

To be sure, some of them are very luminous and some of them are very dim, but that in itself isn't disturbing. We might imagine life developing on a planet that circles an enormously luminous star at a very great distance where the heat and light are diluted by distance and where the far-off giant shines no more brightly than the tame sun in our own sky. Similarly, life developing in the neighborhood of a dim star might do so in its very near neighborhood, catching the necessary heat and light at close range.

There are, however, other shortcomings to take into consideration. The brighter a star, the shorter-lived it is, and the less time there is for life to develop in its neighborhood before the star leaves the main sequence and destroys it all.

No one knows exactly how long it must take for complicated life to develop. Earth assumed its present shape about 4.6 billion years ago. Three billion years later (1.6 billion years ago) life was still primitive, one-celled, and perhaps not very common. We might suppose, then, we would find only those stars useful which would stay on the main sequence *at least* three billion years. That eliminates any star of spectral classes O, B, and A. The more luminous stars of spectral class F are also eliminated.

Let us work from the other end. Suppose Earth were circling a Class M star, such as Alpha Centauri C. It would have to be circling it at a distance of only a million kilometers or so, to get enough energy for life. If it did, however, certain gravitational effects would prove bad for life.

Gravitational pull grows smaller with distance, according to a well-known formula. This means that the side of the Earth facing the sun is pulled more strongly by the sun than the side facing away from the sun. This difference in pull tends to stretch the Earth very slightly in the direction of the sun and produces what are called "tidal effects."

The tidal effect isn't much in the case of the sun-Earth system. The total width of the Earth is only 0.008 percent of the distance from the Earth to the sun, and the gravitational pull of the sun doesn't diminish much over such a small distance.

The tidal effect increases very rapidly as the distance between two bodies decreases. Even a small body close to you can produce larger tidal effects than a large body far away.

The moon is much smaller than the sun and has only 1/27,000,000 the mass of the sun. The moon is, however, only 1/400 as far away as the sun is. That 400 difference in distance more than makes up for the 27,000,000 difference in mass, and the tidal effect of the moon on Earth is twice as great as that of the sun on Earth.

A planet like Earth would have to be circling a Class M star at not very much more than the distance of the moon from the Earth to get enough energy, and the Class M star would be much more massive than the moon. Earth circling a Class M star would therefore experience a far greater tidal effect than it does at present in connection with the sun and the moon.

A tidal effect produces a slowing of a planet's rotation and a large one will, before long, force it to revolve about its sun with one side always facing toward that sun and the other side facing away from it. The one side would be too hot for life; the other side too cold.

We can therefore eliminate any stars of spectral class M as a place whose neighborhood is suitable for life.

That leaves us with suitable stars only among spectral classes G and K, plus a few of the dimmer spectral class F stars.

This is not too bad. Altogether this means that about 1 main-sequence star in 4 is of the right spectral class, or about 30,000,000,000 in our galaxy.

The Habitable Planets

Having a star suitable as an energy supply is useless if there is no planet circling it to receive that energy supply. Do many stars have planets, or is our sun a very unusual exception?

In 1917 the English astronomer James Hopwood Jeans thought the sun was indeed exceptional. He suggested that a planetary system originated only when two stars passed close by each other. The gravitational attraction between them would pull matter out of each one and this star substance would eventually cool down into planets.

If that were so, planetary systems would be very rare indeed. Stars are so far apart, and move so slowly in comparison to their distances, that near-collisions would almost never happen. If Jeans's theory were correct, it might be, then, that the only planetary systems in the galaxy were those of our sun and of the star that nearly collided with it.

Jeans's theory, however, had serious shortcomings. He worked it out before Eddington had shown how hot the interior of a star was. Once Eddington's calculations were accepted, it could be seen that super-hot matter pulled out of a star would just expand into a thin gas. It would never cool into a planet.

Actually, it seems that when a cloud of dust and gas condenses into a sun, it is very common for that cloud to break up into several subclouds and end up as a binary or an even more complicated multiple-star system. Of the stars near us, nearly half are multiple-star systems, and there is no reason to suppose that our own neighborhood is unusual in this respect.

Is it possible, then, that in the formation of stars, the cloud of dust and gas would produce some subclouds so small as to form bodies that weren't large enough to undergo nuclear ignition at the center—in short, planets?

In 1944 the German astronomer Carl Friedrich Weizsäcker (VITES-sek-er) worked out a theory that described the way a cloud of dust and gas contracted. Near the center, the material condensed into a star, but at the outskirts, the dust and gas that lagged behind would swirl in eddies and whirls and in this way form planets. If this theory is correct, then every star as it forms should be accompanied by planets.

Is there any way that this theory can be tested? Can we actually see whether stars have planets or not? Can we see the planets?

Unfortunately, planets don't shine, except by reflected light, and this is too dim to see at the distance of stars, especially since the much brighter light of the stars they circle would drown them out.

Some planets, however, might be detected by their gravitational effects.

A planet and the star it circles move around a common center of gravity. If this center of gravity is far enough from the center of the star, that star would wobble back and forth as seen from Earth, and this would be a sure sign of an accompanying planet, even if that planet were not seen.

In 1844, for instance, Bessel noted that both Sirius and Procyon had such wobbles and he deduced the presence of a "dark companion" for each, a kind of very massive planet. It turned out, in both cases, however, that the companion was a white dwarf, dim enough not to be easily seen, but bright enough to be detected, eventually.

In order for the center of gravity to be a considerable distance from the center of the star, the planet circling it must have a respectable fraction of the mass of the star it circles and must be at a considerable distance from that star. Sirius B, for instance, is about a quarter as massive as Sirius A and is 3 billion kilometers (1.9 billion miles) from Sirius A.

Jupiter, on the other hand, is only 1/1000 as massive as the sun and is only 0.78 billion kilometers (0.49 billion miles) from the sun. The sun's wobble is very small, and if it were viewed from the distance of Sirius it would not be detected at all. And if the presence of Jupiter could not be detected from the distance of Sirius, the presence of Earth, which is far smaller than Jupiter and considerably closer to the sun, certainly could not be detected.

If we are to detect a planet by its gravitational effect on the star it circles, the planet must be considerably more massive than Jupiter, or considerably farther from the star than Jupiter is from the sun, or circling a star that is considerably less massive than the sun—or all three. Furthermore, the star must be quite close to us, or the motion of its wobble wouldn't be large enough to notice.

These conditions are pretty strict. Few stars would qualify, only the near, small ones, and what if they don't happen to have very large planets, just small ones?

Nevertheless, astronomers looked. The Dutch-American astronomer Peter Van de Kamp reported in 1943 that 61 Cygni A (11.2 light-years from us) had a tiny wobble. He decided that a dark body with a mass eight times that of Jupiter was circling 61 Cygni A every 4.8 years. It seemed the easiest way to explain the wobble.

Then in 1960, a planet ten times the mass of Jupiter was reported to be circling Lalande 21185 (8.1 light years away) with an orbital period of ten years. In 1963, a smaller body only 1.5 times the mass of Jupiter was reported to be circling Barnard's star (5.9 light-years away). In fact, continuing studies of Barnard's star's wobble indicate there might be two planets circling it, one the mass of Jupiter, and one the mass of Saturn.

If large planets exist about some particular star, it seems only reasonable to suppose that small planets would exist, too—and be too small to detect by their gravitational effects.

If planets can be detected only under such stiff conditions (small, close stars with large planets circling them at a distance), and yet have been detected for a number of stars, that would seem to bear out Weizsäcker's theory. Most astronomers today are willing to accept planets as the natural accompaniment of stars. Nor need such planets only be circling single stars, since the first planet detected in a system other than our own circled 61 Cygni A, which is part of a binary of which 61 Cygni B is the other member. The planet is therefore called 61 Cygni C.

If, therefore, there are 30,000,000,000 stars in our galaxy that are suitable for life, we might suppose that there are also 30,000,000,000 planetary systems suitable for life.

Life and Civilization

Even if we grant that planets are circling all the suitable stars, are all those planets suitable for life?

Surely not. In our own solar system, there are numerous planetary bodies, but most of them must be barren of anything we can call life. Some are too far from the sun and too cold. Some are too close to the sun and too hot. Some are too small to hold an ocean and atmosphere, without which life cannot develop. Some are so large they have a hydrogen atmosphere, enormous gravities, intense, internal heat, and are in other ways hostile to life.

A planet, to support life, must be just the right distance from its star. It must have a reasonable circular orbit and an axis that has only a moderate tilt to avoid extreme seasons. It mustn't rotate too slowly or it will have extreme day and night temperature.—And so on.

Since the only planetary system we know in detail is our

own, it is difficult to decide what the chances are for a just-right planet to be circling a star. Our own planetary system has exactly one, the Earth, but are we abnormally lucky and are there generally none at all, or are we abnormally unlucky and are there generally several?

In 1963 the American astronomer Stephen H. Dole, making the best estimates he could from the data on our own solar system, thought that perhaps 1 out of 450 or so of the suitable stars would have one planet that could support life. He suggested there might be 645,000,000 habitable planets in our galaxy alone.

And yet a planet may be habitable without being inhabited; it may be suitable for life and yet life may not have developed on it. What are the chances that life will form on a habitable planet? Is it a rare accident, so rare perhaps that it formed only on Earth and nowhere else?

Scientists believe that when the Earth or any Earthlike planet is first formed, it would be rich in substances made up of the light and common atoms. There would be hydrogen itself, and hydrogen in combination with carbon, nitrogen, or oxygen. The combination of hydrogen and carbon is methane, the combination of hydrogen and nitrogen is ammonia, and the combination of hydrogen and oxygen is water.

As it happens, the important molecules of living tissue are made up, for the most part, of hydrogen, carbon, nitrogen, and oxygen. Is it possible, then, that simple molecules made up of these elements on the newly formed Earth gradually became more complex until, finally, they gained the properties of life?

For this to happen, the simple molecules would have had to gain energy, but that is not unlikely. There was energy all around on the early Earth: energy from sunlight, from lightning bolts, from the internal heat of the planet itself, from radioactivity in the crust, and so on.

In 1952 the American chemist Stanley Lloyd Miller experimented with a closed vessel containing water, ammonia, methane, and hydrogen which he carefully sterilized to make sure that no little life forms were included that might introduce chemical changes.

He subjected the mixture to an electric discharge as a source of energy. After a week of this, he found it had turned pink. Analyzing the mixture, he found more complicated molecules than he had started with. Two of them were glycine and alanine, which are simple molecules of the kind out of which proteins are built.

For twenty years other experiments of this sort were conducted, with variations in the starting materials and in the energy sources. Invariably, more complicated molecules, sometimes identical with those in living tissue, sometimes related to them, were formed (though, of course, none have yet been formed that are as complicated as the most complicated chemicals of life— no actual proteins or nucleic acids). All the changes seem to be in the direction of life as we know it.

This was done in small volumes of mixture over very short periods of time. What could have been done in an entire ocean over a period of millions of years?

But is it fair to suppose that what happens in the laboratory is an indication of what would necessarily happen in nature? Perhaps scientists, without meaning to, guide the events and choose the nature of the experiments in such a way as to get the results they expect.

We can't go back in time to see what really happened on the early Earth, but occasionally small bodies from outer space strike the Earth. Friction heats them up to the melting point as they streak through the atmosphere, but if they are large enough, some of the object will survive to reach Earth's surface as a meteorite. Such meteorites are as old as the Earth and represent a sort of time machine. Their chemistry might represent what Earth was like before life came.

Most of the meteorites are made up of rocks, or of metal, and don't contain the kinds of elements out of which life could have developed. A certain rare kind of meteorite, however, the carbonaceous chondrites, *does* contain such light elements.

Two such meteorites have fallen in recent years. In 1950 one fell near Murray, Kentucky; in 1969 another fell near Murchison, Australia. Both were collected and studied by scientists before they could become contaminated with material from Earth's soil. It turned out that each contained carbon atoms in combination with hydrogen and occasional other atoms that resembled the sort of arrangements in the molecules found in living tissue. The same sort of changes that had taken place in the laboratory had also taken place in those meteorites.

Then there are the clouds of dust and gas to be found in outer space between the stars. These clouds give out radio waves (like light but with much longer wavelengths) and, from the wavelengths we receive, the nature of the molecules in the clouds can be worked out. In the 1970s, over a dozen different molecules have been detected, most of them containing carbon atoms in combination with hydrogen, nitrogen, or oxygen.

It would seem, then, that there is a strong tendency for the simple molecules to become more complicated even under unfavorable conditions. It can happen in clouds of dust and gas in space, and in meteorites, so surely it can happen on the surface of a planet such as the Earth. Interestingly enough, all the changes that have been observed are in the direction of our kind of life, and not of some form of life with a basically different chemistry.

It seems reasonable to conclude, then, that on every habitable planet life will form, and that it will always be our form of life. By Dole's calculations there ought to be 645,000,000 life-bearing planets in our galaxy alone.

But how many of these life-bearing planets are occupied by a species of living creature intelligent enough to build a civilization?

We have no way of telling. All we can say is that our own

planet is 4,600,000,000 years old, according to the best estimates, and has had a civilization on it for, at most, 10,000 years, if we count from the time some people began to build primitive cities. That means that, as of now, a civilization has lasted on Earth for only about 1/500,000th of its history.

We don't know whether this is typical. Civilizations may appear sooner on some planets, later on others. They may last for millions of years or may destroy themselves in mere thousands. But suppose we assume we are average in this respect and decide that one out of every half a million life-bearing planets bears a civilization.

In that case there would be about 1,300 civilizations in our galaxy alone (and, of course, over a million billion of them if the other galaxies are taken into account).

These civilizations may be at various stages of advancement. If we assume ourselves to be average in this respect, too, there may be 650 civilizations in our galaxy that are more advanced than we are.

Locating Other-World Life

Naturally, we are more interested in life-bearing planets than in dead ones, and more interested still in life-bearing planets with advanced civilizations. If such civilizations exist, can we tell where?

So far we cannot.

Superior civilizations might come out exploring and might reach us, but so far they haven't. Of course, there are frequent reports of "unidentified flying objects" and enthusiasts believe these represent such exploration. If so, however, nothing has come of it, and except for "eye-witness" reports, riddled with hoaxes, errors, and confusion, there is no evidence. Erich von Däniken, in his book *Chariot of the Gods*, maintains that such exploring teams visited Earth in prehistoric times, and his writings have gained great popularity among the unsophisticated, but his suggestions cannot be taken seriously.

If superior civilizations stay at home, or just explore their own immediate planetary system, they may still send out signals of some sort that we might pick up. As a matter of fact, astronomers have, every once in a while, scanned the sky to see if there might be some sort of radiation that has a suspicious set of regularities about it, as though it were being sent out with the deliberate intention of arousing interest. No such radiation has yet been detected, but human efforts have as yet been minor.

Suppose we decide to make an intense and long-sustained search of the sky in an attempt to pick up any signals that might be there. Are there any places where we ought to concentrate our attention?

We can do a lot of eliminating. For instance, the farther the source of radiation, the weaker it is when it reaches us. From a very distant source, a civilization would have to be sending out radiation with impossibly high intensities in order to have it reach us in an identifiable way.

Then, too, the farther a life-source was, the longer the time it would take its signal to reach us. A signal from the nearest large galaxy outside our own, the Andromeda galaxy, would take 2.3 million years to get to us. And, of course, any answer we sent would take another 2.3 million years to get back. Even a message from the center of our own galaxy would take 30,000 years to get to us.

It would seem, then, that the practical consideration of energy and time would tell us that we ought to concentrate on the stars in our immediate neighborhood.

Within about 16 parsecs (52 light-years) of ourselves, there are perhaps 2400 stars. Of these one-fourth, or 600, ought to be of the right spectral class to possess, possibly, a habitable planet. By Dole's calculations, one out of 450 of such stars should indeed possess a habitable planet, so that we have reason to expect that there is a habitable and life-bearing planet within 16 parsecs of ourselves. (There are perhaps even two or

three if we are lucky—but perhaps none at all if we are unlucky.)

Naturally, the chances of there being a civilization that close
could be extremely small if we stick with the assumption that
only one out of every half a million life-bearing planets had
developed one. The assumption, however, might be wrong. Perhaps civilizations are as inevitable as life itself, and wherever
there is the possibility of a life-bearing planet, the signals of a
civilization ought to be searched for.

Well, then, which of the stars within the 16-parsec limit ought
we to concentrate on? Usually the decision is to pick stars
which, like the sun, are single and are not part of multiple-star
systems, which are as near the sun's spectral class (G2) as
possible, and which are as close as possible.

The nearest single star of the same spectral class as the sun
is Zeta Tucanae. It is 7.1 parsecs (23.3 light-years) away from
us. There are three single stars closer to the sun than Zeta
Tucanae is, but they are distinctly smaller and cooler than the
sun (yet not too small or cool to have a habitable planet). These
are listed in Table 38, where Alpha Centauri A and Alpha Centauri B are also included for comparison.

TABLE 38

Nearby Sunlike Stars

| STAR | SPECTRAL CLASS | LUMINOSITY (SUN = 1) | DISTANCE | |
			PARSECS	LIGHT YEARS
Zeta Tucanae	G2	0.9	7.14	23.3
82 Eridani	G5	0.7	6.20	20.2
Tau Ceti	G8	0.4	3.62	11.8
Epsilon Eridani	K2	0.3	3.28	10.7
Alpha Centauri B	**K2**	**0.3**	**1.34**	**4.40**
Alpha Centauri A	**G2**	**1.0**	**1.34**	**4.40**

Ordinarily, in discussions of the detection of signals from other planets, the Alpha Centauri system is not mentioned. Yet notice that Alpha Centauri A is just as much like our sun as Zeta Tucanae is, if not more so, and it is at only a fifth the distance from us. What's more, Alpha Centauri B is very much like Epsilon Eridani and is at only two fifths the distance of that star from us.

Why not investigate the Alpha Centauri system as the possible home for life and civilization? (Naturally, we eliminate Alpha Centauri C from consideration.)

The only objection to this is that Alpha Centauri A and Alpha Centauri B form a binary system and, in this way, are drastically unlike the sun.

This, however, may not be a fair objection. Binary systems can also have planetary systems. The 61 Cygni binary has at least one planet circling 61 Cygni A, and it could be that each of the two stars has a planetary system. The same could be true of the Alpha Centauri system as well.

It might be argued, of course, that the presence of a second star might make conditions on a planet too extreme, produce a too elliptical orbit, introduce harmful temperature extremes.

This need not be so. If Alpha Centauri B were introduced into our solar system and made to circle the sun instead of Alpha Centauri A (see page 103), then clearly planets circling in the orbit of Jupiter and beyond would be very much interfered with by the new star and its gravitational field. The planets in the inner solar system, including Earth, would, however, be too close to the sun to be much disturbed by Alpha Centauri B.

Dole argues that both Alpha Centauri A *and* Alpha Centauri B might have an inner planetary system equivalent to our own system out nearly to the orbit of Jupiter, and that in each case this would not be interfered with too badly by the companion star. Each of the stars would then be capable of having a habitable life-bearing planet circling itself. (There might also be relatively far-distant planets that circle the center of gravity of the two stars, rather after the fashion of Alpha Centauri C. These are likely to be too far out to be habitable, however.)

Dole calculates what the chances are that each of several of the nearest stars may have a habitable planet. He finds six stars in the near neighborhood of the sun which have, in his analysis, about 1 chance in 20 (0.05 probability) of possessing a habitable planet. These stars are given in Table 39.

Of these six most likely stars, Alpha Centauri A and Alpha Centauri B are by far the closest, but that is not their only advantage. The other four are in different directions, and to go from any one of them to any other would involve a trip light-years in length. Alpha Centauri A and Alpha Centauri B, however, are part of the same system. To go to one is to be within planetary distance of the other. It is the only case, of those listed in Table 39, where two stars may be investigated in a single trip, so to speak.

We must, therefore, ask what the chance is that either Alpha Centauri A or Alpha Centauri B will have a habitable planet. Dole estimates this to be in the range of probability of 0.107, or better than 1 in 10.

TABLE 39

High-Probability Habitable-Planet Stars

	DISTANCE	
STAR	PARSECS	LIGHT-YEARS
Alpha Centauri A	**1.35**	**4.40**
Alpha Centauri B	**1.35**	**4.40**
70 Ophiuchi A	5.31	17.3
Eta Cassiopeiae A	5.52	18.0
Delta Pavonis	5.89	19.2
82 Eridani	6.20	20.2

Of the nearest stars with a chance of possessing habitable planets, then, the Alpha Centauri system is not only by far the closest, but also has the highest probability. Certainly, then, if we are going to investigate stars for habitability, life, and civilization, the Alpha Centauri system ought to stand at the head of the list.

Of course, there is no sign in any of the observations of the Alpha Centauri system that suspicious signals of any sort are originating in it, but that is not something to be surprised at.

A civilization, even if it exists, may not be sending out signals, or may be sending signals of a nature we do not recognize. Then, too, even if a civilization does not exist, the Alpha Centauri system might yet contain a habitable planet, bearing life of a sort not capable of constructing a civilization. Even that would be enormously interesting.

In the absence of signals, we may never be able to observe whether or not there is a habitable planet in the Alpha Centauri system, unless we actually go there. Can we carry through such a visit?

The Alpha Centauri system is 4.40 light-years distant. That means it would take a beam of light 4.40 years to cross the vacuum between ourselves and Alpha Centauri, and then another 4.40 years to come back to us. Scientists are quite convinced now that no material object can travel faster than light, so that astronauts making the round trip cannot be away from home for less than 8.80 years no matter what they do.

(Some scientists have speculated that it is possible for particles to exist that always go faster than light. If so, they might conceivably be harnessed to make trips between the stars much shorter than they would otherwise be. Actually, though, these superfast particles have not yet been detected and there are some scientists who argue that they cannot exist.)

Naturally, ships will not take off instantly at the speed of light. Nor, going at the speed of light, will they stop instantly in the Alpha Centauri system. Nor will they want to turn about instantly as soon as they reach Alpha Centauri and make for home. Instead, there would be a period of acceleration to higher and higher speeds until some maximum is reached, then a period of slow deceleration to lower and lower speeds until Alpha Centauri is reached. There will then be a period of exploration, after which the return voyage will be made in a similar acceleration-deceleration way.

Such a trip is not likely to take less than twenty years all told, from the standpoint of the people waiting on Earth.

Even if a twenty-year voyage is acceptable, the period of acceleration and of deceleration would consume a great deal of energy and it is doubtful (barring some great advance in technology) whether a spaceship can carry a large enough energy source to supply what is needed for the purpose.

Suppose, instead, that acceleration is used to build up some reasonable speed and that the ship is then allowed to coast all the way. No energy is required for the coasting though, of course, energy would still be needed to operate the life-support system on the spaceship.

Some of the rockets sent out by human beings in the last twenty years or so have moved through space at speeds as high as 18 kilometers (11 miles) per second. Let us suppose that we can build a ship that will attain ten times that speed—180 kilometers (110 miles) per second—and that it can then be allowed to coast in the direction of the Alpha Centauri system. How long will it take the ship to reach the neighborhood of Alpha Centauri?

It will take 7,400 years! Then, of course, after a period of exploration, it would take another 7,400 years for the ship to return to Earth.

If the ship had started in the time of the biblical patriarch Abraham, it would be only a little more than halfway to Alpha Centauri right now.

Reaching Alpha Centauri won't be easy, therefore, and reaching any of the other, still more distant, stars will obviously be more difficult still. In fact, unless some unexpected break-throughs in technology are made, people from Earth may never go to Alpha Centauri or to any of the other stars.

On the other hand, if space colonies are ever established, each carrying tens of thousands of human beings, those space colonies may be fitted out with some advanced space drive and they may then take off for the stars. The colonists aboard won't care how long such a voyage takes since they will be taking their home with them—but then they will very likely never return to Earth.

Still— It is hard to see the future. The time may come when the stars may be easily reachable by some method now unfore-seen. And if so, it is very natural to predict that the first stars to be explored will be those of the Alpha Centauri system.

It may even be that if either Alpha Centauri A or Alpha Cen-tauri B has a habitable planet with no native intelligent life forms, human beings will colonize that planet. The Alpha Cen-tauri system will then be the first place where human beings will be making a new life for themselves under a strange sun.

GLOSSARY

ABSOLUTE MAGNITUDE—The magnitude a star would have if it were located ten parsecs away from us.

ALANINE—A substance with molecules that contribute to the makeup of proteins.

AMMONIA—A substance with molecules made up of a nitrogen atom and three hydrogen atoms.

ANGLE—A figure formed when two straight lines meet at a point or when two planes meet along a line.

APASTRON—The point of greatest distance of separation of two stars circling each other.

ASTRONOMICAL UNIT—The average distance of Earth from the sun; about 150,000,000 kilometers.

ATOM—A particle of matter made up of a central nucleus surrounded by electrons.

ATOMIC NUCLEUS (plural, ATOMIC NUCLEI)—A tiny structure at the center of the atom, containing almost all the mass of the atom.

AXIS OF ROTATION—The imaginary straight line about which an object spins.

BASE LINE—The change in position from which you view the same object in determining its parallax.

BINARY STARS—Two stars that are close together in space and that revolve about each other.

CARBONACEOUS CHONDRITE—A meteorite containing carbon atoms and other light atoms.

CELESTIAL EQUATOR—An imaginary circle about the sky, lying exactly above every point on Earth's equator.

CELESTIAL LATITUDE—The angular distance north and south of the ecliptic.

CELESTIAL POLES—Imaginary points in the sky that are directly above Earth's north and south poles.

CELESTIAL SPHERE—The sphere formed by the sky as it appears to us.

CELSIUS SCALE—A way of measuring temperature, in which water freezes at 0 degrees and boils at 100 degrees.

CENTER OF GRAVITY—The point about which two bodies move as each revolves about the other.

CONSERVATION OF ENERGY—The ability of the energy of the universe to change its form but never to decrease or increase in quantity.

CONSTELLATION—A grouping of stars in the sky, often pictured in some familiar shape.

DECLINATION—The measure in degrees of distance north or south of the celestial equator.

DEGREE—An angular measure equal to $\frac{1}{360}$ the circumference of a circle.

DENSITY—The mass of an object divided by its volume.

DIAMETER—The length of a straight line passing through the center of a geometric shape or an astronomical body.

DOPPLER EFFECT—The change in the pitch of sound when its source is moving either toward us or away from us.

DOPPLER-FIZEAU EFFECT—The change in wavelength of light when its source is moving either toward us or away from us.

DOUBLE STARS—Two stars that appear to be close together in the sky.

ECCENTRICITY—The degree to which an ellipse is flattened and the distance changes of a circling object from the object it circles.

ECLIPTIC—The plane that passes through the center of the sun and through all points of Earth's orbit.

ELECTRON—A subatomic particle found in the outskirts of the atom.

ELLIPSE—A curve that looks like a flattened circle.

ENERGY—That property of an object which makes it possible for it to do work.

EQUATOR—The circumference that lies halfway between the two poles of a spinning object.

FOCUS (plural, FOCI)—One of two points inside an ellipse. The two foci are at equal distances from the center of the ellipse and on opposite sides, along the major axis.

GALAXY—A huge collection of from millions to trillions of stars. In particular, the collection of which our sun is part.

GLYCINE—A substance whose molecules contribute to the make-up of proteins.

GRAVITATION—The attraction exerted by one object on the other objects in the universe.

HELIUM—A gas composed of the second simplest of all atoms; always present in stars.

HYDROGEN—A gas composed of the simplest of all atoms; it forms the main constituent of stars of the main sequence.

HYDROGEN FUSION—The forcing together of four hydrogen nuclei to form a helium nucleus; an energy-yielding process that powers our sun and other stars on the main sequence.

INTERFEROMETER—A device that can measure the manner in which two beams are not quite parallel to each other.

KILOGRAM—A measure of mass equal to about 2.2 pounds.

KILOMETER—A measure of length equal to about ⅝ of a mile.

LATITUDE, PARALLELS OF—Imaginary east-west lines parallel to the equator on Earth or to the celestial equator in the sky.

LIGHT-YEAR—The distance light travels in a year, about 9,500,-000,000,000 kilometers.

LONGITUDE, MERIDIANS OF—Imaginary north-south lines stretching from pole to pole of a rotating body.

LUMINOSITY—The comparative brightness of objects at fixed distances from the observer.

MAGNITUDE—The apparent brightness of an object shining in

the sky. The brighter the object, the lower are the figures which represent the magnitude.

MAIN SEQUENCE—Those stars, making up the majority of those we see, which are of normal size and brightness—neither giants nor pygmies.

MAJOR AXIS—A diameter passing through the foci of an ellipse; the longest diameter of an ellipse.

MASS—In a general way, the amount of matter in an object.

METEORITE—A small body from space which has collided with Earth's solid surface.

METHANE—A substance with molecules made up of a carbon atom and four hydrogen atoms.

MINOR AXIS—A diameter at right angles to the major axis of an ellipse; the shortest diameter of an ellipse.

MINUTE OF ARC—An angular measure equal to $\frac{1}{60}$ of a degree.

MOLECULE—A group of atoms held together more or less permanently.

NEBULA—A cloud of dust and gas in space.

NEUTRON—A subatomic particle, not carrying an electric charge, found in the atomic nucleus.

NEUTRON STARS—Tiny stars, smaller than white dwarfs, that can be only ten kilometers in diameter yet are as massive as full-sized stars.

NITROGEN—A type of atom essential to life. It makes up $\frac{4}{5}$ of the atmosphere of Earth.

NUCLEAR FUSION—The forcing together of small atomic nuclei to form somewhat larger atomic nuclei.

NUCLEIC ACID—A large molecule, made up of many atoms, that is characteristic of all life forms.

ORBIT—The path taken by an object revolving about another object.

ORBITAL PERIOD—The time it takes for one object to complete one turn about another object.

OXYGEN—A type of atom essential to life. It makes up $\frac{1}{5}$ of the atmosphere of Earth.

PARALLAX—The apparent change of position of a close object

compared to a more distant object, when the viewer shifts the position from which he views the object.

PARSEC—The distance at which an object would show a parallax of one second of arc; about 3.26 light-years.

PERIASTRON—The point of closest approach of two stars circling each other.

PERIOD OF REVOLUTION—The time it takes for one object to complete one turn about another.

PHASES—The different shapes of the lighted part of a planet or satellite shining by reflected light from a star.

PLANET—A body that circles a star and shines only by reflected light.

PRISM—A rod of glass with a triangular cross section.

PROPER MOTION—The motion of a star in the sky, resulting from its own motion relative to the other stars.

PROTEIN—A large molecule made up of many atoms and characteristic of all life forms.

PROTON—A subatomic particle, carrying an electric charge, found in the atomic nucleus.

RADIAL VELOCITY—The speed of motion of a star directly away from us or directly toward us.

RADIOACTIVITY—The slow but steady breakdown of certain atoms, which give off energy and radiation in the process.

RED GIANT—A star that is enormously large in volume and has a rather cool surface temperature.

RED SHIFT—The change in position of spectral lines toward the red end of the spectrum when, for instance, the light source is moving away from us.

REVOLUTION—The circling of an object about another object.

ROTATION—The spinning of an object about its own central axis.

SECOND OF ARC—An angular measure equal to $\frac{1}{60}$ of a minute of arc.

SPACE VELOCITY—The speed of motion of an object through three-dimensional space, relative to ourselves.

SPECTRAL CLASSES—Groups of stars resembling one another in the general appearance of their spectra.

SPECTRAL LINES—Lines that cross a spectrum: either dark lines against a bright background, or bright lines against a dark background.

SPECTROSCOPE—A device used to form a spectrum of a star or of some other glowing object.

SPECTROSCOPIC ANALYSIS—The determination of the chemical structure of an object by studying the exact position of its spectral lines.

SPECTROSCOPIC BINARY—Two stars circling each other at such small distances that they look like a single star even through a telescope, but which are revealed as two stars by the motion of their spectral lines.

SPECTRUM (plural SPECTRA)—Light that has been spread out so that each different wavelength is in a different position, as in a rainbow.

STAR—A mass of matter much larger than a planet, within which nuclear fusion takes place causing it to grow hot and glow with light.

STELLAR EVOLUTION—The changes that take place in the properties of stars as time goes on.

STELLAR PARALLAX—The parallax of a star.

STELLAR SPECTRA—The spectra of stars.

SUB-ATOMIC PARTICLES—The tiny particles that, taken together, make up an atom, together with other particles of similar size.

TELESCOPE—A tube containing lenses, mirrors, or both, which makes distant objects look larger, nearer, and brighter.

TELESCOPIC DOUBLE STAR—Two stars close enough to look single to the eye alone, but which through a telescope are revealed as double.

TEMPERATURE—The intensity of heat.

TERNARY STARS—Three stars, close together, that form part of a single system.

TIDAL EFFECTS—Those effects produced by the difference in the gravitational pull on one side of a body from that on the other side.

TRANSVERSE VELOCITY—The speed of motion of a star across our line of sight.

VOLUME—The room taken up by any object.

VIOLET SHIFT—The change in position of spectral lines toward the violet end of the spectrum when, for instance, the light source is moving toward us.

WATER—A substance with molecules made up of two hydrogen atoms and an oxygen atom.

WAVELENGTH—The length of a wave; particularly of a wave of light or of light-like radiation.

WHITE DWARF—A pygmy star, no larger than a planet but just as massive as a full-sized star.

ZODIAC—A band of twelve constellations circling the sky; and within which the sun, moon, and planets seem to move.

INDEX

About the Author

ISAAC ASIMOV says he writes about anything that interests him. In more than 170 books and hundreds of articles and short stories, he has entertained and enlightened readers on every branch of science and a wide variety of other subjects, including mathematics, language, Shakespeare, the Bible, poetry, humor, mysteries, and science fiction.

Born in Russia, he came to the United States at the age of three and spent his childhood devouring not the candy, but the books and magazines in his father's stationery store in Brooklyn, New York. At Columbia University he earned the degrees of B.S., M.A., and Ph.D., and then joined the teaching staff of Boston University, where he still holds the title of Associate Professor of Biochemistry in the School of Medicine.

A noted wit and raconteur, he is in great demand as a speaker, and has received countless awards and honors, including honorary doctoral degrees. He and his wife live in a New York City apartment with a telescope and an unobstructed view of the skies.